The Not So Log

CABIN

Robbin Obomsawin

Gibbs Smith, Publisher
Salt Lake City

The Not So Log

CABIN

Robbin Obomsawin

Log-Element
Building & Design

First Edition
07 06 05 04 03   5 4 3 2

Text © 2003 by Robbin Obomsawin
Photograph copyrights noted throughout

Published by
Gibbs Smith, Publisher
P.O. Box 667
Layton, Utah 84041

Orders: (1-800) 748-5439
www.gibbs-smith.com

Project directed by Suzanne Gibbs Taylor
Edited by Monica Millward Weeks
Designed and produced by Kurt Wahlner and Rick Harris
Printed and bound in China

Library of Congress Cataloging-in-Publication Data
Obomsawin, Robbin, 1960-
The not so log cabin / Robbin Obomsawin. — 1st ed.
v. cm.
Contents: The not so log cabin — What your mother never told you about
contractors — Design 101 — How much does a custom home cost to build?
— The secret to building perfection — The good, the bad, and the ugly
— Building for a lifetime.
ISBN 1-58685-152-7
1. Log cabins. I. Title.
TH4840 .O26 2003
690'.837 — dc21

2002015987

Note from the author: The stock plan designs and construction blue-
prints in this book are all copyrighted.
No portion of this book or any drawing may be reproduced, modified, or
reused without permission from the copyright owner.

Reproducible master plans can be purchased with a license — although
still limited to single construction-project use —
that permits modifications to be made to the plan and allows for up to
twelve copies of a plan for use in building a single home.

Even if you purchase a license to make modifications to a copyrighted
design, modified designs are not released or free from the original designer's copyright. Please respect design copyrights, as the purchase of these
plans enables us to produce this book.

The information in this book is intended to motivate and enrich the read-
er's thinking. It is not a guide for building. The drawings in this book are
not to be construed as construction drawings nor may the descriptions
contained within be presented to or relied upon by any engineer, architect, designer, or construction professional.

The methods, designs, and details shown in this book are not intended to
be appropriate in all situations and should be assessed and
verified by a qualified professional, ensuring their safety, durability, and
appropriateness for the individual situation and compliance with applica-
ble codes and regulations. The author and publisher bear no responsibility
for any outcome resulting from practical application
of any idea in this book.

Contents

© 2003 Custom Log Homes.

Acknowledgments

First, I want my boys Jarred, Jason, and Jimmy to know that I appreciate their help and support with cooking, cleaning, typing, spell checking, designing floor plans and layouts, photographing, and keeping the log yard up and running since I have spent so much time locked in my office.

A special thanks to my sisters-in-law, Lizza Obomsawin and Marion Dickerman, who have spent many late nights and long days reading notes, general text, and ideas about construction, content, structure, and reworking it to build a book all the more understandable for the public. I appreciate their willingness to do whatever it took often with very little notice or with short timelines.

I am grateful for the years of support and encouragement from my mother- and father-in-law, Elizabeth and Raymond Robert Obomsawin, who are always there with helping hands no matter how busy they are.

As always, thought and consideration go to my parents, Jim and Esther Whitman, who instill in me an understanding and consideration for others as well as a healthy respect for the world and the notion that in some small way we can make a difference.

To my husband, Jules Obomsawin, who always works so hard and is always willing to share his natural talent as a log builder to build the dreams of so many of our clients. He is like the postman . . . where nether rain, nor sleet nor snow will stop him from delivering a client's dream. We have often designed the impossible just to test Jules' skills, but we find that he has only tested our skills.

Many thanks to my editor, Suzanne Taylor, and Gibbs Smith, Publisher for allowing me to share my experience in the wild world of handcrafted log construction. They have also been very supportive of craftspeople who are so often misunderstood and under appreciated. Suzanne's guidance, input, and creativity-along with her team of publishing elves - are what brings this book to life!

Introduction

Your own home — the stuff that dreams are made of! Building a custom home is often a long-awaited dream. For many, this dream includes a log home, but it's not always practical to build a log home from the ground up. Fortunately, you don't need a log home to evoke the romance of log home living — you can incorporate log elements in a new or existing home, creating the same feeling for a fraction of the cost and effort. The purpose of *The Not So Log Cabin* is to inspire you, the homeowner, to think outside the box and allow you to create a rustic spin on a new style of "log" home revised for modern-day lifestyles. With so many material choices possible that are as varied as the people who live in them, log-element structures provide a limitless style of construction. This new hybrid of architecture reflects the pioneering spirit of today's unique and adventurous builder.

The Not So Log Cabin is filled with tips, hints, and techniques that will help you sort through the options to realize your dream. A variety of styles of log-element homes

Years of hard work, ingenuity, and dedication have formed this design, whose finish components are created from reclaimed materials. Salvaged or reclaimed woods are regaining respect and appreciation from homeowners and builders, which has come from a heightened sense of responsibility to protect our valuable natural resources.

© 2003 Conklin Authentic Antique Barnwood.

are featured throughout, from grand estates to cozy outbuildings, from classic Adirondack camps to homes of the Wild West. A number of house plans will help you visualize the design possibilities, while beautiful color photographs throughout showcase homes that have incorporated log elements with breathtaking results.

Whatever your tastes and budget, you are certain to find a style that pleases you, as well as guidance for achieving that style, within the pages of *The Not So Log Cabin*.

The bumps and jogs of this whole-log post-and-beam structure are incorporated into a nook with a log ladder leading to a loft with tree house charm. This must be the most popular kids' hangout ever—a permanent fort right inside the house! The changing angles of the roofline, with doubled log purlins and ridgepole with dark-stained ceiling boards, are a great contrast to the white stucco walls.

© 2003 Rocky Mountain Log Homes

Chapter One

Basics of Log-Element Structure

Many people, because of their way of life and sense of adventure, are drawn to distinctive types of architecture that are influenced by nature. The not-so-log cabin is a new hybrid of architectural style that integrates a home with nature, using any design approach from the most primitive rustic style to extreme contemporary. Borrowing from many traditional methods creates a new style of log construction called log-element or whole-log post-and-beam construction, or, if you will, a not-so-log cabin. (Log-element construction is the way we easterners prefer to call this hybrid style as the term *post-and-beam* in its strictest definition means a traditional timber-frame or old-world style of square timber construction.)

This cedar-sided clapboard home has a stone base designed in a Craftsman style. The log elements in the roof system beautifully balance the visual weight of the stone skirt below.

© 2003 Roger Wade

What Is Log-Element Construction?

The not-so-log cabin begins with conventional construction framing methods enhanced by the use of log elements, "twig art" detailing, and often a kiss of log whimsy. The combination of log elements can be used in roof systems, floor joists, stairs, railings, and support columns within a conventionally built structure, giving the home a tree house charm. The mixtures of these methods create a dramatic contrast of rustic logs against more delicate conventional materials, packing a punch in artful craftsmanship. The high contrasts of a log-element home is for those who want to incorporate rustic elements of nature without living in a traditional log home.

This unique home can be a blend of sophisticated styles. Regional distinctions of log-element construction have been around for decades, seen in New England or old-world–vintage timber-frame cottages; Adirondack twig art within its great camps (built at the turn of the century), which were modeled after Iroquois longhouses with the utilization of bark sheathing and free-form application of natural materials; western prospectors' log cabins carved out of the nearby woods; traditional southwestern adobe structures with log corbels, *vigas*, and *latillas*; and traditional Scandinavian scribing techniques.

These unusual combinations of whole-log elements will certainly provide a more casual feel than more formal traditional timber-frame structures. This form of building is not just limited to new construction; it can easily be incorporated into an older home's renovation plan. Log-element construction provides a look of natural simplicity or casual log elegance with a level of sophistication for timeless appeal.

The march of large log columns stands at attention at this home's entry hall. The mix of log columns, floor joists, and log girders is a striking feature that creates rustic glamour in this log-element structure. The soft lines and sensuous curves of the sweeping staircase carry the eye to the second-floor loft, where windows flood the stairs with natural light.

© 2003 Roger Wade

What Are the Advantages of Incorporating Log Elements in Your Home?

This new hybrid of architectural styles presents a pioneer spirit through an earthy blend of natural materials that redefines rustic. A log-element structure is an organic sculptural design with distinctive architectural flavor and irresistible rustic charm, in which nature becomes the central force of its design. Log elements can be combined in any number of ways for an artful and eclectic mix of rich and varied building styles that create a casual grace, merging function with beauty. For example, materials may be combined to integrate contemporary elements with classic traditions. The log-element home has flexibility and a dramatic flair that evokes an atmosphere desirable to the country soul in all of us.

The lower costs involved with incorporating log elements (as opposed to log-wall construction) are also appealing. A new conventionally built home can be enhanced with logs for a fraction of the cost of building an entire log-wall (or shell) structure, and even existing homes can benefit from the addition of log elements, making it possible for more people to enjoy the warmth and natural beauty of cabin design.

The large-diameter log scissors truss appears to grow out of the conventional wall. Engineering and design go hand in hand when log trusses, purlins, and structural components are incorporated into a conventionally framed home.

© 2003 Steve Mundinger, Charles Cunniffe Architects

This is an example of how a log railing interfaces with a log column for a smooth transition and a tight fit. The mortised and tenoned cedar log rails have added strength and durability.

© 2003 Beaver Creek Log Homes

The rhythm of trusses creates a covered porch that makes a statement and provides a grand entry to this stone structure. Even the windows are framed in log accents. A good design can make an area more dramatic or subtle based on the materials, colors, and proportions used.

Squared purlins and valley rafters contrasted with the whole-log post-and-beam frame add a layer of texture.

© 2003 Roger Wade

The use of log elements at the entry draws the visitor with clear direction to the main door. Decorative trusses, log columns, log railings, and cap logs can add a great deal of personality to a modest-sized home. The use of several outdoor covered porches and open decks creates a home whose multifunctional space can accommodate large gatherings while retaining the coziness that is just right for intimate conversations.

Beautiful kitchens do not have to be big! This pint-sized kitchen packs a punch in color as well as function. The space is a well-planned use of every inch. Vintage-style cabinetry and design give the room an Early American flair.

The pure artistry of this talented Adirondack craftsman has transformed a hum-drum small camp into a work of art. The log accents are concentrated into the camp's entry, creating a home with distinctive Adirondack style. The entry porch's log treads are slabs of cedar, carefully scribed into the base platform. There is also a cedar bench cleverly disguised into the far set of railings.

© 2003 Ugene Slade

Chapter Two

How to Incorporate Log Elements in Your Home

Log columns, trusses, and railings can be configured into an endless number of design ideas, depending on the combination of client, design professional, builder, and log artisan. In this home, final additions such as lights, furniture, and accessories are just as important as the home's general design, creating a fluid feel and continuity that capture this rustic glamour and lend a tailored contemporary spirit to the home.

© 2003 Roger Wade

Log-element construction is similar to log-wall construction in that the building methods' joinery techniques are more complex than in conventional building. However, with an experienced builder, log elements can be incorporated in your home easily and effectively. Consider the following issues when preparing to add log elements to a new or existing house.

How Does Log and Log-Element Construction Differ from Conventional Construction?

The art of handcrafted log construction is a centuries-old form of timber construction that primarily utilizes hand-held tools such as axes, chisels, and scribers. These methods have not changed over hundreds of years, although some power-assisted tools such as chain saws, electric sanders, grinders, and heavy equipment for moving the full-length logs have been added to help speed up this labor-intensive form of construction. Even with this added help, the work involved is tedious. A lead time of six months to one year is not uncommon in the hand-crafted trade to allow the handcrafters to prepare the log elements. Many crafters may also be booked years in advance. If you cannot afford a conventional home, you will likely not be able to afford a log-element home. The perception that the log-element home should be the same cost as a conventional home is, unfortunately, more of an illusion than a reality. The truth is that log-element architectural details are labor-intensive to

The builder cuts a majority of the log work in the log builder's yard, but some cuts are needed on-site to accommodate unforeseen obstructions or something as simple as needing one more inch for the tile work to fit underneath the log columns. With log-element construction, it is important to have plans that are tailored for this style of construction. Even a few inches can require a drastic change in the type of cut or support needed in a particular location, and can affect the quality of joinery and the finished look achieved.

The general contractor and crew install the roof's 2 x 6 tongue-and-groove decking over the log purlins when the log trusses are being installed on the home's entry. This V-groove decking becomes the ceiling as well as support for the SIPs (structural insulated panels) that rest on top of this vaulted ceiling's deck.

© 2003 Beaver Creek Log Homes / Trout House Village

During the construction process, you can see the V-groove decking boards that run from ridge to wall over the log purlins, becoming the ceiling. The builder makes cuts into the upright conventional columns that help support the log purlins and ridgepole.

Insetting log stubs into the stonework of the fireplace allows the builder to scribe a log mantel that fits the bumps and curves of the stonework. The resulting mantel appears seamless—you cannot tell where the log or stone begins or ends. Log mantels can be designed in a wide range of styles and tastes.

© 2003 Beaver Creek Log Homes / Trout House Village

create. Log-element construction is a very customized form of building, one not conducive to manufactured mass-production techniques. If you choose to build a log-element structure, you should build this style because you prefer the added architectural interest and warmth that natural log elements radiate. Log elements incorporated into a home can generally add anywhere between 5 and 30 percent to the home's overall cost of construction, depending on the design, complexity, and quality of connection methods used. The added costs will be for the extra log-element details such as stairs, floor joists, trusses, and railings.

Adding Log Elements to Your Home

A variety of log elements can be added to the interior and exterior of your home. Some are most easily integrated while building a house, while others could be added to an existing home at any time. Some of the most popular log elements added to homes include the following:

Log trusses, which form the roof's log framework, are the ultimate in log joinery and show the builder's experience, knowledge, and artistry. The incorporation of trusses into a conventional roof system can be jaw dropping if done well. It can create a cathedral of nature's spiritual overtones.

This grand entry has an asymmetrical design created with a lot of stone, clapboard siding, log newels and railings, dormers, and a tower room.

© 2003 Roger Wade

Log rafters are a beautiful focal point when used in the main structure of the porch or dormer's roof system. The graceful rhythm of the log rafters makes a striking feature. They can be added to an existing home's porch where you would like to transform a humdrum house into a home with rustic drama. A combination of log rafters within the main roof system with supporting purlins is also a striking mixture. There is nothing plain or boring when log rafters are used.

This designer chose reclaimed and recycled woods for everything from the walls, ceiling rafters and recycled ceiling boards, to the re-planed old floorboards and railings to add charm and whimsy that reflect the designer's sense of humor.

Purlins, the horizontal beams that support a roof's system, can be used on their own, providing added interest within the roof system. If purlins are used in combination with log trusses, however, the magical mix of rustic components will create a dazzling dance of log work overhead. If purlins are used alone in a vaulted ceiling, then added hidden supports will need to be incorporated into the gable ends. Long-spanning vaulted roof systems will need to be carefully considered and engineered into the home's design.

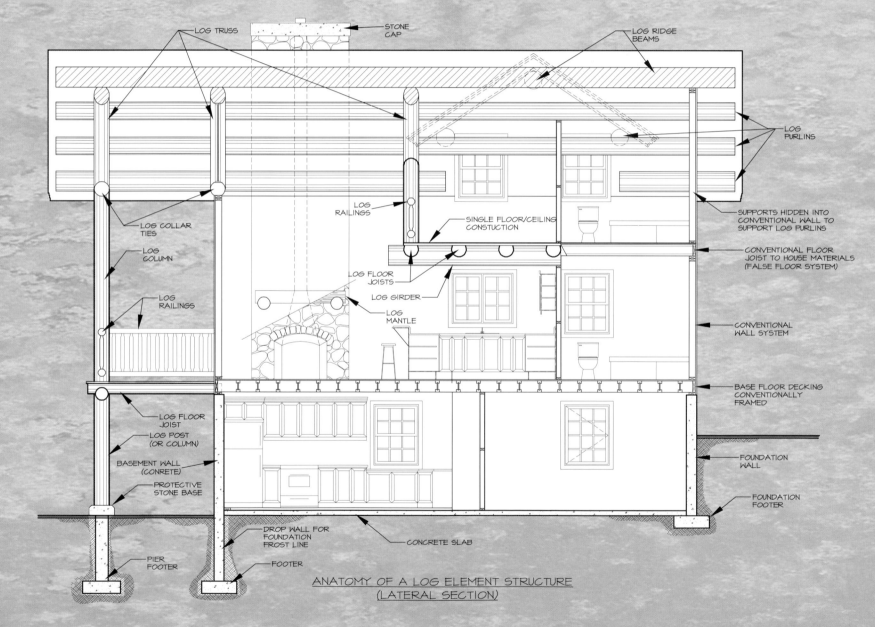

ANATOMY OF A LOG ELEMENT STRUCTURE
(LATERAL SECTION)

Floor joists, the beams that usually support the second floor, can present a dramatic flair within a log-element structure. The massive log joists give the home a sense of permanence and security. They provide a very solid floor system from above as well as a magnificent ceiling from below (called **ceiling joists** when viewed from below). These joists can be more costly if you need to add a conventionally framed floor on top to house all the mechanicals.

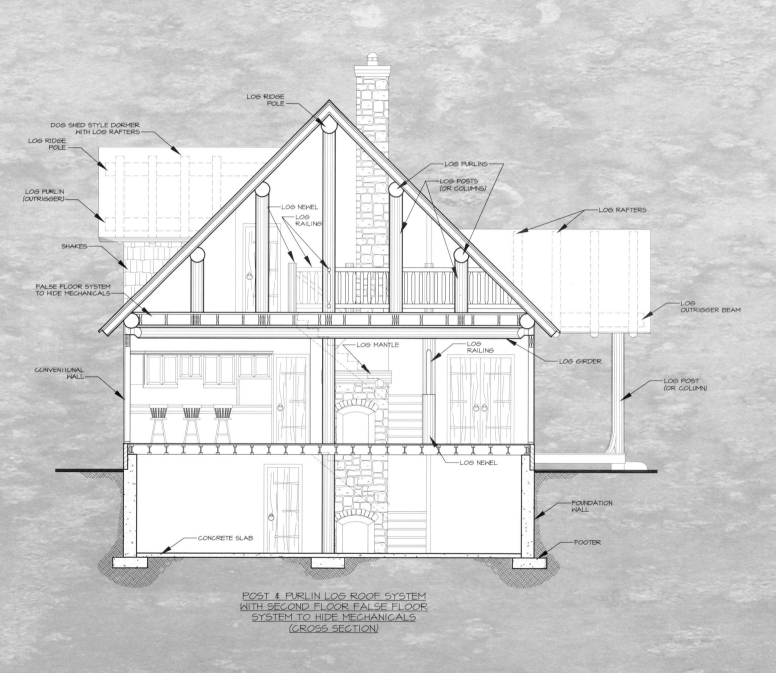

LOG RIDGE POLE

DOG SHED STYLE DORMER WITH LOG RAFTERS

LOG RIDGE POLE

LOG PURLINS

LOG POSTS (OR COLUMNS)

LOG PURLIN (OUTRIGGER)

LOG NEWEL

LOG RAILING

LOG RAFTERS

SHAKES

FALSE FLOOR SYSTEM TO HIDE MECHANICALS

LOG OUTRIGGER BEAM

LOG MANTLE

LOG RAILING

CONVENTIONAL WALL

LOG GIRDER

LOG POST (OR COLUMN)

LOG NEWEL

FOUNDATION WALL

CONCRETE SLAB

FOOTER

POST & PURLIN LOG ROOF SYSTEM
WITH SECOND FLOOR FALSE FLOOR
SYSTEM TO HIDE MECHANICALS
(CROSS SECTION)

Log railings flanking the stairs, loft areas, or porches can be a staple in log-element construction. Just the presence of traditionally constructed log rails or free-form twig-art–style railings can fill a home with architectural interest as well as add punch and personality to an exterior design. The variation and combinations of log railing styles are endless. You can create or design your own, but a standard well-built set of railings can be just as spectacular.

STANDARD

CATTAILS

PINE TREES

ROUND

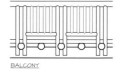
HEARTS

TWIG ART

"V"

CIRCLES & DIAMONDS

GRID

WEB

ARROWS

BALCONY

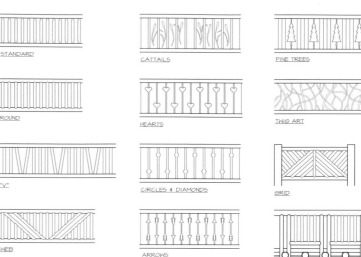

Log stairs can become a beautiful focal point and provide a high contrast against a conventionally built wall system. Straight, spiral, or winding stairs will enhance the overall architectural design of the home. The grace and rustic charm of a well-designed set of stairs is undeniably noticeable, providing texture and depth to a home.

The log elements of this stair system contrast with the plaster and faux-suede–finished walls. The large log stringers support the log treads that you climb. The base of the log railings is fully scribed with a round-on-round connection, with a double top handrail. Although the stairs and railings have a simple traditional feel, the joinery methods are very complicated—not the luck of a novice log builder.

© 2003 Charles Cunniffe Architects / Steve Mundinger

The major log-element feature in this conventionally built home is the gracefully spiraling log staircase with log railings. These artfully built stairs even have a log stringer (tastefully selected for its natural curve), where the log treads are anchored for support. The rails are all mortised into the handrails and shoe rails for added strength.

A large log floor joist supports the second floor. Under the floor joist is a main girder and log columns. The structure's frame was built with conventional 2 x 4 and 2 x 6 construction methods with a standard Sheetrock finish.

The twig art sculptural design incorporates the Lake Placid Lodge name into the balcony railing system, creatively welcoming all to the main lodge.

© 2003 Lake Placid Lodge

Log Styles

The following pictures demonstrate some of the hybrid styles of log-element architecture or post-and-beam construction. The homes of three distinct North American regions are highlighted. All three styles of log-element homes use inspirational combinations of logs, stone, and glass that echo the spirit of their distinctive regions.

Adirondack Twig Art Structures

Adirondack twig art uses the natural bends and twists of wood to create sculptural design in sync with nature. These Adirondack structures also integrate layered textures, incorporating other natural and indigenous materials into artistic forms to create the magical feel of the Adirondacks. These elements are sculpted to blend in with the surrounding land, while keeping with the Adirondack tradition of disturbing nature as little as possible.

The sense of warmth and storybook charm are evident in this log-element structure. This cozy setting is part of the Lake Placid Lodge, built in the late 1800s in a classic Adirondack style of log-element or whimsical twig art features of construction.

Southwest Tradition of Log-Element Construction

This timeless style of construction embraces three cultures in the American Southwest: Native American, Hispanic, and Anglo. Mud, straw, sticks, and stones are creatively sculpted into homes that blend in with their high desert surroundings. The use of log *vigas* (purlins) and *latillas* (smaller twig latticework) are used to support the roof systems. Many of these traditional buildings have survived the march of time and are still in use. The legacy of long-ago traditions still lives in the architecture today, where each door of a southwestern-style home has a story to tell.

The following sections will highlight a variety of house plans and completed homes that incorporate some of these details and styles.

Southwest chic is captured in this design with the tradition of round log columns, which support decoratively carved corbels with a large-diameter squared timber header that supports the long distance between columns. The use of adobe-style walls with curving edges, wrought iron, niches, doorway arches, large hand-made tiles, vegas, and latillas (the lattice work of small log saplings used in the roof system) are all part of the classic southwest sculptural design and artistry.

© 2003 Roger Wade

Cowboy Chic

The American and Canadian West is the heart of cabin fever, where modern-day pioneers of the new frontier of log construction are always willing to think outside the box of the log cabin's four walls, turning cabins into castles. From western Canada down to the southwestern United States, today's cowboys of log construction are building grandiose-style "cabins" of the Wild West.

© 2003 Roger Wade

This log-element structure demonstrates the contrast, artistry, and rhythm of log placement as well as the mix of materials. The dark log work accentuates the white walls in the whole-log post-and-beam—style structure. The wrought-iron railings contrast gracefully with the log work and white walls.

© 2003 Roger Wade

Log purlins and ridgepoles that run the length of the structure make up the second-floor roof system. A dormer incorporates more log supports, which add interest to the design. There is a set of central log columns with ridge support that transfers the roof load to the floor below.

© 2003 Roger Wade

Log-element structures often use log ceiling joists or floor joists. Recessed lighting, mechanical plumbing, and heating can hide in this area with the use of a "false floor" system.

© 2003 Roger Wade

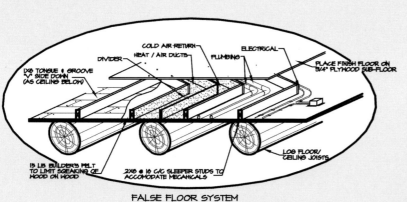

COLD AIR RETURN
HEAT / AIR DUCTS
DIVIDER
ELECTRICAL
PLUMBING
1X6 TONGUE & GROOVE
"V" SIDE DOWN
(AS CEILING BELOW)
PLACE FINISH FLOOR ON
3/4" PLYWOOD SUB-FLOOR
15 LB BUILDER'S FELT
TO LIMIT SQEAKING OF
WOOD ON WOOD
2X6 @ 16 C/C SLEEPER STUDS TO
ACCOMODATE MECAHICALS
LOG FLOOR/
CEILING JOISTS

FALSE FLOOR SYSTEM

Building a false-floor system hides all construction mechanicals. You can construct a false floor by using 2-inch x 2-inch strapping (also called "sleepers") up to a 2-inch x 12-inch conventional floor joists system throughout the entire second floor. This conventional framing or "skeletal" system allows you to run HVAC duct work, plumbing, electrical wiring, and lighting into these cavities. This is a more expensive option than just laying down floorboards over the log floor joists, but it is a solution that can house the elements needed for modern-day conveniences.

Kitchens do not have to be in all-wood tones in a log-element house. Painted cabinets and white walls contrast with the natural-element construction. The robin's-egg blue color creates a light and airy feel.

© 2003 Crown Point Cabinetry

Outdoor spaces extend living quarters and allow for beautiful views of stonework and natural elements like those o the following pages.

© 2003 Rob Melnychuk

A well-built stone wall can become a beautiful addition to a home or help retain a steeply sloping site. Attention to detail often makes a house work well with its surroundings.

This gardener made the most of his rocky terrain and created a true *rock garden*. Some of the most difficult sites can become treasures by working with, instead of against, the obstacle.

The general contractor and crew install the roof's 2 x 6 tongue-
and-groove decking over the log purlins while the log trusses are
being installed on the home's entry. This V-groove decking becomes
the ceiling as well as support for the SIPs (structural insulated
panels) that rest on top of this vaulted ceiling's deck.

Above: © 2003 Beaver Creek Log Homes / Trout House Village
Opposite: © 2003 Timmerhus, Inc.

The grand entry focuses on log elements, where the timber-frame truss has a functional but decorative center king post with side struts. The truss's collar-tie, or base cord log, is seated on a plate beam, with a knee brace supporting underneath.

© 2003 David O. Marlow

Overleaf:

Log elements highlighted in the ceiling of this home are contrasted nicely against the conventional walls. Rustic stone elements are also applied to the fireplace surround, complementing the natural log elements.

© 2003 Charles Cunniffe Architects

Richly textured marble surfaces are incredibly durable while aging gracefully over time. The kitchen, once hidden behind closed doors, has now evolved into the primary room of the home, or "command central."

Earthy materials such as stone, tile, wood floors, and log elements like those in the free-form log stairs, log-column supports and overhead log girders all add to this home's rustic elegance.

© 2003 Murray Arnott Design Ltd.

Oversized log columns are used as log accents that also become structural supports for the overhead roof load. The wall of glass is anchored at the corners by the use of these massive timbers.

© 2003 Murray Arnott Design Ltd.

Chapter Three

Classic Cabins

Log home lovers are often drawn to the traditional images remembered from childhood, such as a small snow-covered cabin on the edge of the woods with smoke rising from the chimney. The designs in this chapter were planned to evoke such feelings of nostalgia, featuring traditional log elements such as purlins, trusses, and rafters, while maintaining a simplicity of form in the structures themselves.

This living room incorporates a good balance of log elements. The "web" truss is filled with glass while the floor-to-ceiling windows are framed with log columns and log beams. This design is wrapped in windows that bring the outdoors in.

© 2003 Rob Melnychuk

Bug Hill

Living area: 1,015 sq. ft.
Basement: none
Decks and porches: 254 sq. ft.

Bedrooms: 2
Bathrooms: 1

FRONT ELEVATION

Bug Hill has a simple classic beauty. The plan is simple and cost-effective. This is a home that is perfect for the first-time buyer or a small family, or as a great vacation home. It is fluid and flexible in design, with plenty of closets and storage space to house all those cabin provisions.

The exterior base is wrapped in an Arts & Crafts architectural style. The wainsboard exterior siding gives the home rustic appeal.

Inside, the home has a large kitchen, with a built-in breakfast bar/work area creatively tucked into a bay window. The living room/dining room has space for the warmth of a fireplace.

Log-Element Features

The entry log columns and log rafter roof system enclose a very comfortable and useful outdoor room, creating a place you never want to leave. The home also incorporates large log ceiling joists throughout.

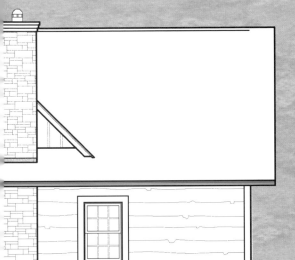

ELEVATION

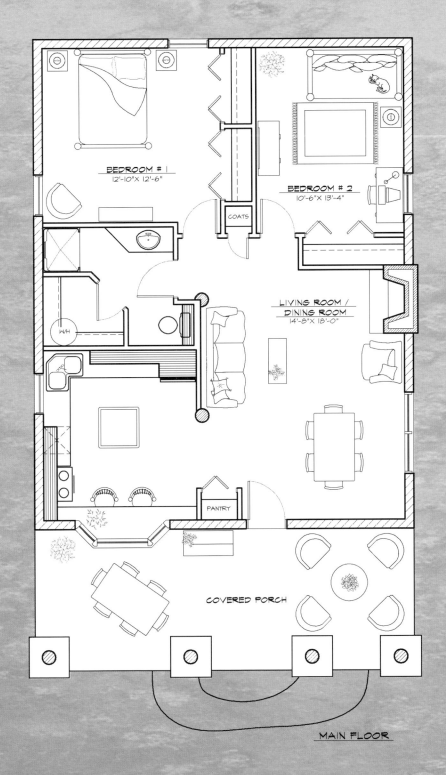

BEDROOM # 1
12'-10" X 12'-6"

BEDROOM # 2
10'-6" X 13'-4"

COATS

LIVING ROOM /
DINING ROOM
14'-8" X 18'-0"

W/H

PANTRY

COVERED PORCH

MAIN FLOOR

This child's bedroom is what dreams are made of. The carved bear-post beds, lamps, accessories, and details are not too hard—or too soft—but just right. Structural elements, such as the log ridgepole and purlins, add visual balance to this whimsical home in the trees.

This shingle-style home's grand entry uses logs in the columns, trusses, and door transom area to create a home that welcomes all who enter.

Camp Singing Bear

Living area: 1,575 sq. ft.
Basement: 902 sq. ft.
Decks and porches: 429 sq. ft.

Bedrooms: 3
Bathrooms: 2

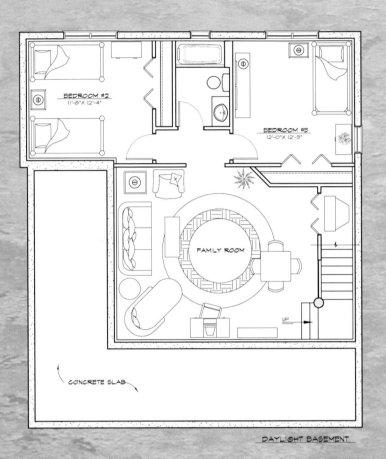

DAYLIGHT BASEMENT

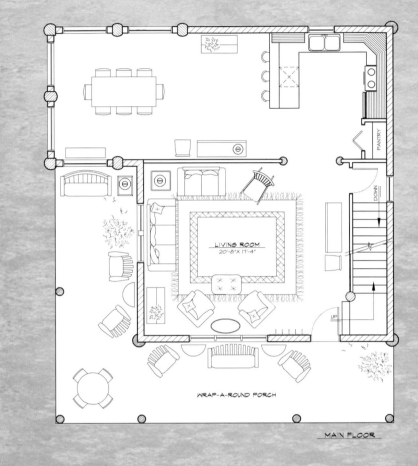

MAIN FLOOR

This is the essence of a fairy-tale cabin with cottage charm. A tower room adds a touch of whimsy to this magical home. Even though Camp Singing Bear is contained in a small footprint, it makes good use of every inch of space. While this home appears to be simple in form, it is not for the novice builder. This small package is packed with complex log joinery.

The main floor contains all the public living spaces, where proportions are grand in size. The kitchen has a breakfast bar that overflows into a dining room wrapped in windows for a sunroom effect. Upstairs, the loft is a romantic master suite that includes a walk-in closet and a wonderful spa-style bathroom. This master retreat will provide a bit of vacation without leaving home.

The daylighted basement is a private area, with plenty of design flexibility and ample closet space. This secluded one-floor unit provides kids with a sense of independence while hiding all the flying debris that seems to follow them around.

Log-Element Features

The first-floor ceiling joists are located throughout the main floor and create a dramatic feel. Log rafters above the bump-out of the dining room area create a lot of architectural interest in this room's design. The roof system is full of log purlins that are anchored by a mix of hidden supports and log columns.

The American-traditional wraparound porch with log rafters looming above it suits this cabin plan just fine.

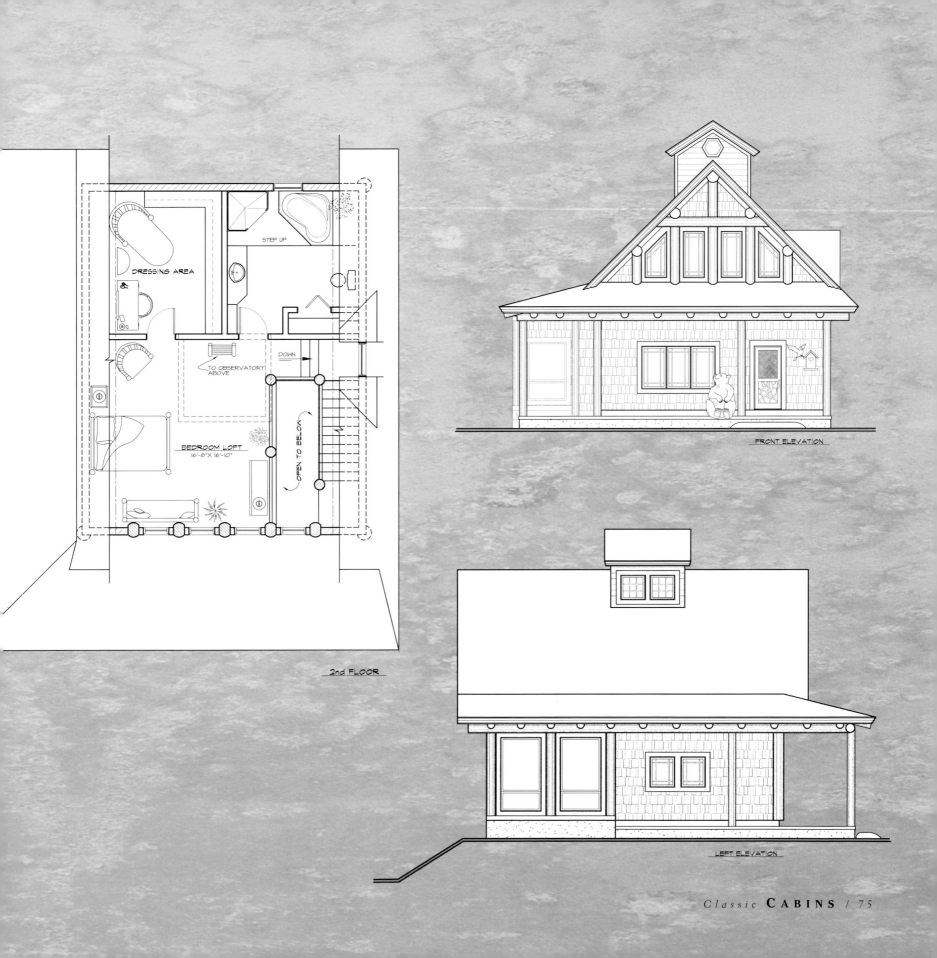

STEP UP

DRESSING AREA

TO OBSERVATORY!
ABOVE

DOWN

OPEN TO BELOW

BEDROOM LOFT
16'-8" X 16'-10"

2nd FLOOR

FRONT ELEVATION

LEFT ELEVATION

This home incorporates a masonry stove that has a pizza/bread oven on one side toward the kitchen and a fireplace on the living room side. The fire heats benches that wrap around three sides. This efficient fireplace system allows only a little wood to heat a whole house on even the coldest days. The centrally located masonry chimney mass makes the most of the radiant heat. You may hear this type of heating system referred to as a Russian stove, Swedish fireplace, or masonry heater.

© 2003 Beaver Creek Log Homes

Subtle log elements barely hint at their structural functions. The atmosphere of log-element homes can range from light and airy to dark and dramatic.

© 2003 Rob Melnychuk

The double log girder adds design interest. This kitchen's knotty pine cabinets with a clear finish give a light and monochromatic effect to the room.

© 2003 Roger Wade

Camp Sunflower

Living area: 2,268 sq. ft.
Basement: 1,232 sq. ft.
Decks and porches: 468 sq. ft.

Bedrooms: 4
Bathrooms: 3-1/2

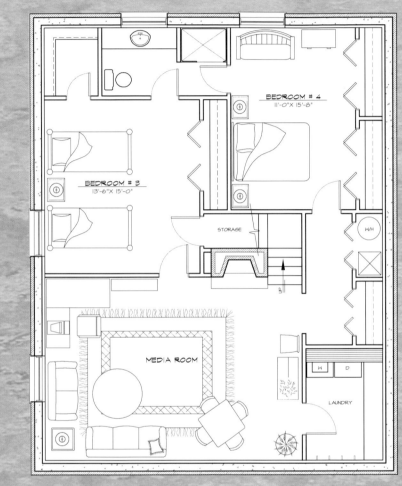

DAYLIGHT BASEMENT

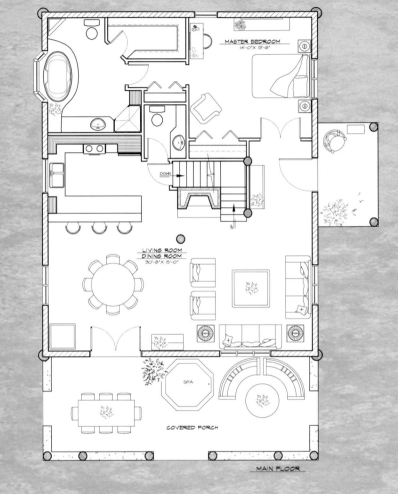

MAIN FLOOR

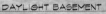

Camp Sunflower is a classic four-corner structure, designed with plenty of room for a large family.

The main floor's master bedroom suite is loaded with luxury, featuring a large soaking tub tucked into a small bay window that wraps the bather in nature. Upstairs is a large bedroom with a loft perched over the living room below and its own bathroom. The daylighted basement has two more bedrooms with a shared bathroom, plenty of closets, a laundry room, and a large media room with a full-sized fireplace.

The large side porch is an added outdoor great room that extends the living space, perfect for an outdoor barbecue.

Log-Element Features

The entry is built with a graceful log scissors truss that draws one in. The side porch is a massive, beautiful log (or timber) truss system that adds great architectural interest to this home.

There are a lot of log ceiling joists incorporated into the first floor's ceiling that, in turn, support the floor system for the second story. The main roof system is made up of log purlins that have support posts hidden in the wall system.

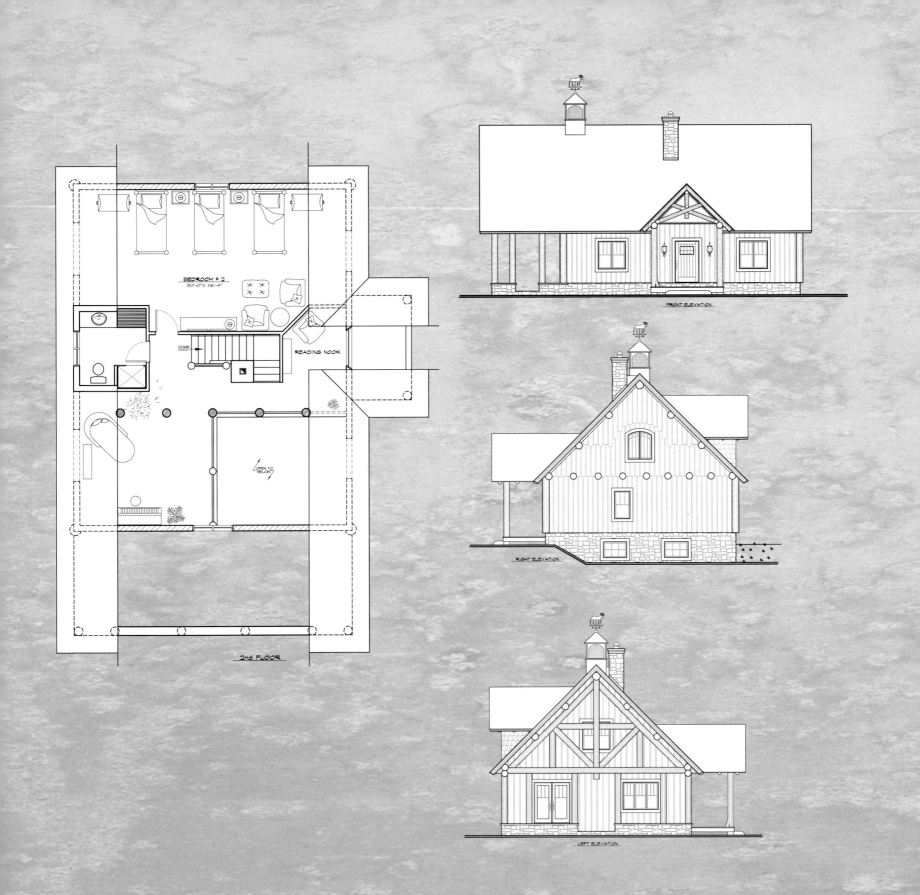

BEDROOM # 2
30'-0"X ±16'-4"

DOWN

READING NOOK

OPEN TO BELOW

2nd FLOOR

FRONT ELEVATION

RIGHT ELEVATION

LEFT ELEVATION

The use of painted cabinets of butter yellow, a painted breadboard on the walls, and a stainless-steel sink area combine for a fresh and bright kitchen.

© 2003 Crown Point Cabinetry

This casual kitchen has a homegrown style with some open shelves to display collections. The structural log headers above the doors and windows add beautiful architectural detail.

© 2003 Roger Wade

Camp Thistle Wood

Living area: 2,080 sq. ft.
Basement: 1,248 sq. ft.
Decks and porches: 279 sq. ft.

Bedrooms: 3
Bathrooms: 3

FRONT ELEVATION

REAR ELEVATION

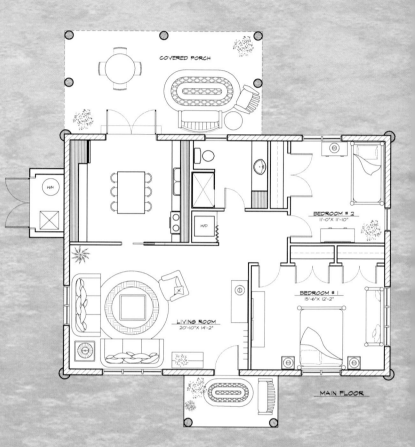

COVERED PORCH

BEDROOM # 2
11'-0" X 11'-10"

BEDROOM # 1
15'-6" X 12'-2"

LIVING ROOM
20'-10" X 14'-2"

MAIN FLOOR

The plan for Camp Thistle Wood features classic shingle-style architecture that is pure and simple with no fuss about it, perfect for respite in a secluded hideaway. The hip-roof system is a classic feature of shingle-style design that softens the cabin's hard edges.

The modest square footage is well utilized to allow the most efficient living space while maintaining a comfortable flow of rooms. Although small in size, this cabin is cost-effective by design. It is a home that easily accommodates first-time homebuyers, empty nesters, or vacationers.

Log-Element Features

A sunburst pattern of log work crowns the entry of this classic shingle-style cottage design. The back-porch truss has a symmetrical line of log spindles that all stand at attention like soldiers guarding the gate. The flat ceiling is enhanced by rustic log beams looming overhead.

Copper Mountain

Living area: 1,519 sq. ft.
Basement: none
Decks and porches: 526 sq. ft.

Bedrooms: 3
Bathrooms: 1

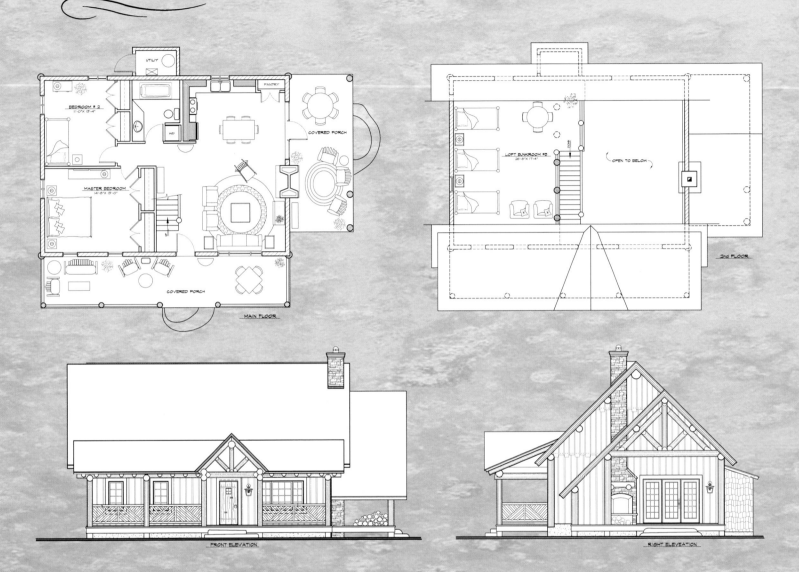

Copper Mountain is a cottage with a classic design and feel. Variations in the rooflines add character to this distinctive home. With subtle changes to the choice of railings, roof pitch, or exterior finish materials, this house becomes a chameleon of styles.

The peaked covered porch directs visitors to the front entry. The amenity of multiple large porches enhances the design's appeal. The indoor/outdoor fireplace is the focus of the vaulted roofline.

On the interior, a sense of spaciousness makes this log home as dramatic inside as it is outside. A sweeping loft overlooks the living room below. The loft can be a great bunk room for additional guests, an office, or a craft room.

Log-Element Features

The structural log elements of purlins, trusses, and rafters in the roof system are exposed for all to enjoy. The main-entry shed porch is made with log rafters, while the side porch is a mix of purlins and a truss. Log railings are a main feature—on the front porch, up the stairs to the loft, and across the length of the loft.

Porch railings are one of the most common places to feature twig art. This railing resembles artwork inspired by traditional Adirondack craftspeople.

Log elements and accents are even used within the furnishings of most Adirondack camps. Birch bark and twigs are coveted for their changing tones of bark depending on the species of wood chosen. It is the combination of these materials artfully arranged that becomes the trademark of the craftsman.

Loon Island Cottage

Living area: 648 sq. ft.
Basement: none
Decks and porches: none

Bedrooms: 1
Bathrooms: 1 with outdoor shower

FRONT ELEVATION

RIGHT ELEVATION

LIVING ROOM
15'-4"X 13'-8"

BEDROOM
10'-0"X 12'-6"

UTILITY

BENCH SEAT

LINEN

BENCH

OUTDOOR SHOWER

MAIN FLOOR

This home is tailored for vacation living where simple is the rule, with space only for cabin provisions. Although small, it is an efficient use of space with a built-in dining nook, galley kitchen, and an extra outdoor shower to create a home with vacation style. The bedroom could easily be made into a bunk room to sleep four or six with bunk beds. The small footprint becomes a great escape from the larger vacation homes.

The cabin's exterior has a playful element no matter what finish materials are chosen. Oversized plates of windows wrap around two sides of the living area to capture the sweeping views, integrating the outdoors with the indoors. The home's hip-roof design creates cottage charm and a timeless beauty and ambiance.

Log-Element Features

The log entry is this home's focal point. The log work within the entry, as well as the exterior materials used, can transform the look and feel of this house. There are beautiful log ceiling joists incorporated into the flat ceiling system within the living room, kitchen, and bedroom.

Pine Meadows

Living area: 1,545 sq. ft.
Basement: none
Decks and porches: 222 sq. ft.

Bedrooms: 2
Bathrooms: 2

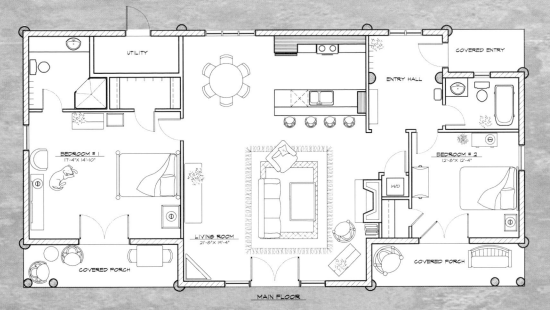

MAIN FLOOR

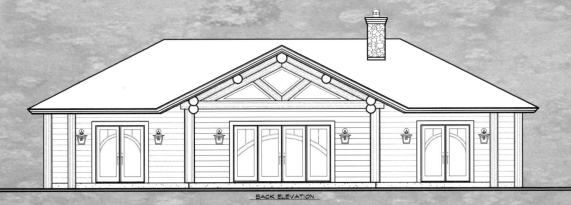

BACK ELEVATION

Pine Meadows incorporates several porches to relax on during a sunny day or starlit evening. The design feature of the hip roof is a striking system that gracefully fits the scale and proportion of this home.

This cabin is designed for one-floor living, with chic style and a calming environment. The large elegant entry hall welcomes all who enter, and has enough space for one to sit down to remove outdoor gear. The open forum of the public living area is a great place to entertain friends and family.

Log-Element Features

The living room ceiling vaults up to large-diameter log trusses above, while the rest of the ceilings have log joists that give the rooms distinctive architectural interest and rustic appeal.

The porch system's ceilings could easily incorporate small log *latillas* to add a rhythm of visual interest and depth into the porch overhead.

The mix of country French furnishings, hickory chairs, a forest green island, and reclaimed wood floors gives this home a cottage charm with a fusion of high styles.

© 2003 Rocky Mountain Log Homes

A creative gardener made a focal point out of this abandoned farm seeder. The mixture of color and texture is a feast for the eyes.

Chapter Four

Taking Cues from Nature

With a whimsical mix of "sticks and stones," this log-element structure's center columns were carefully chosen for the natural branching structure of the tree. A sequence of log rafters placed closely together lends a dramatic look and substantial feel to the log-element roof system. The stone bases flare to balance the flow of the home's design. Although small, this home has the voice of a grand estate.

© 2003 David O. Marlow

The Adirondacks have perhaps the richest legacy of camp-style living of anywhere in the world. Images of fishing in a cool lake on a warm summer's day or wandering a rocky path through the forest, then retreating to a comfortable cabin in the evening, fill the thoughts of those who seek Adirondack living. With their emphasis on nature, these homes fulfill the vision of anyone seeking their own slice of mountain paradise, whether in the Adirondacks or the Rockies.

One typical feature of Adirondack-style homes is twig art, which is fashioned into everything from wall hangings to porch railings. These homes also include natural flourishes such as bark-on railings and porches to enhance outdoor living.

Camp Blue Wolf

Living area: 1,432 sq. ft.
Basement: 794 sq. ft.
Decks and porches: 854 sq. ft.

Bedrooms: 2
Bathrooms: 2

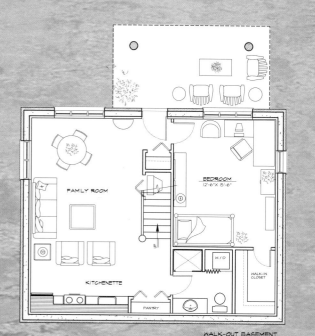

WALK-OUT BASEMENT

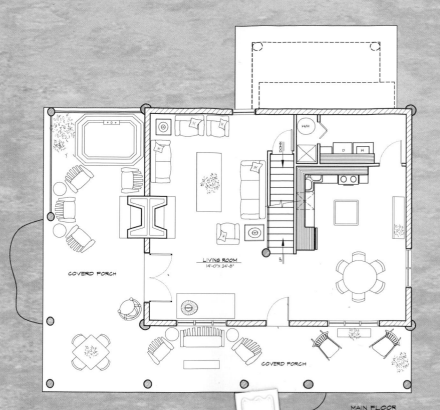

MAIN FLOOR

This unique and charming home creates a stimulating atmosphere with its Adirondack twig-art doors, railings, and wainsboard Adirondack siding. The home overflows with porches for great outdoor living, including an outdoor fireplace deserving of marshmallows and ghost stories.

The home is centered around the main-floor living room, which is very large and warmed by the glow of a fire. The second floor has a hint of fantasy in the master bed-room suite, with its built-in Swedish-style bed and space to build in a headboard shelf for books. The bunk area has a set of windows that make this a magical playhouse once the curtains are closed for privacy. This elegant suite also has its own private reading loft that overlooks the living room below.

Using space efficiently is also a trademark of this plan. For example, the second-floor bathroom is carved out of the bump-out dormer, creating a larger space.

The bonus of a walkout basement makes for a great in-law suite, guest apartment, teenage retreat, caretaker's apartment, or home office.

Log-Element Features

The two-sided covered porch protecting the entry porch with log railings and the side porch with a truss and purlins that extend from the main roofline are the outdoor areas where log elements are featured. The main roof system is built with a post and purlins as well as a beautiful timber-frame truss located in the home's center.

Looking inside, there are large-diameter log floor joists visible throughout the first-floor ceiling system in the living room and kitchen. Free-form twig art is used within the railing system throughout the home, providing a classic Adirondack flavor.

2nd FLOOR

MASTER BEDROOM
16'-4" X 19'-8"

BUNK

OPEN TO BELOW

DOWN

LINEN

LOFT

LEFT ELEVATION

BACK ELEVATION

FRONT ELEVATION

These Adirondack-style townhouses blend into their mountain environment at the base of the Aspen Mountains. The architect carefully considered each inch of space to create a luxurious environment with an old-lodge feel that evokes the mountain spirit of the Colorado Rockies.

The architect captured the power and complexity of log-element construction with a carefully considered design and quality logs, and chose an experienced and talented log builder who could interpret the complicated connections to create a finished product that is simply stunning. The log scissors truss and even the log railings show the builder's skills. The mix of colors and use of textures in the home's exterior materials create visual interest, while the Adirondack palette of tan, brown, sage, and forest green help the home blend into its surroundings.

© 2003 Charles Cunniffe Architects

This outdoor living area is a tranquil space with distinctive style. The angled fireplace and sharp-edged corners combine to create a contrast between the home and nature.

© 2003 Roger Wade

Doubled log columns in this log-element townhouse lend a sense of strength and security. The column tops are scribed with round-on-round connections to the main log girder above so that the logs appear to grow out of one another. The flagstone entry, stone fireplace, and dark wallpaper contrast with the logs nicely.

© 2003 Charles Cunniffe Architects

Camp Dragonfly

Living area: 1,499 sq. ft.
Basement: none
Decks and porches: 1,600 sq. ft.

Bedrooms: 4
Bathrooms: 2

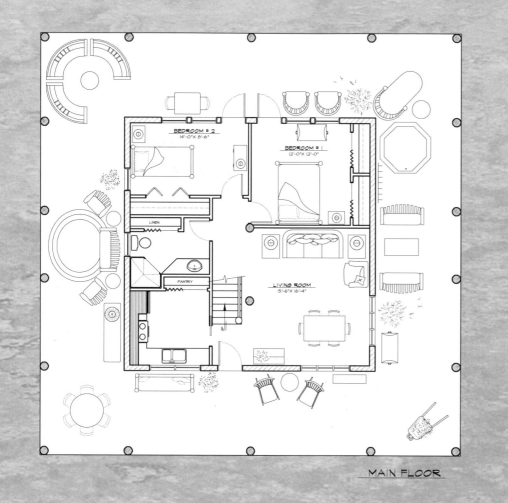

MAIN FLOOR

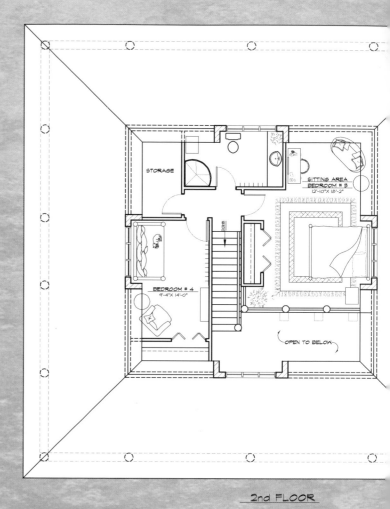

2nd FLOOR

This four-gable-style camp is an Adirondack classic, a home with story-book charm. Randomly placed shingle siding along with scallop-cut shingles in the dormer peaks add to this home's dramatic dimensions. Camp Dragonfly also lends itself to outdoor comfort — the wraparound covered veranda is a porch-lover's dream.

Within the home, the layout is compact but efficient. The main floor has two bedrooms that could easily be made into one large suite. The kitchen has a pocket door, so you can close off a mess in the kitchen if unexpected guests drop in. An upstairs loft has a large bedroom that over-looks the living room below.

Log-Element Features

The four-sided porch is loaded with log rafters that are supported by whimsical log columns, hand-selected for their natural character and charm.

The roof system is a mass of intersecting log purlins and ridge-poles that create the most spectacular dance of logs overhead. The second-floor loft is carried by a mix of log girders and log floor joists that, when the log joinery is done well, create connections that look as though they grew out of one another. Logs are incorporated into the stair railings and the loft's bedroom perch.

FRONT ELEVATION

REAR ELEVATION

The "rules" of Adirondack design require you to build with materials found on the surrounding property. From rawhide lamp shades and birch-bark furniture veneers to bark waste barrels, the art of building in the Adirondack tradition, influenced by the Iroquois and Algonquin Indian cultures, is still in vogue today. The mountain architecture and twig artistry in this home showcase a sophisticated but rustic style that wins the hearts of all who enter.

© 2003 Jon Prime / Adirondack Store

Oversized log columns dramatize the home's entry with natural imperfections called checks. Checks occur where changes in temperature and humidity cause cracks in logs. This occurrence is considered part of the appeal of a log-element structure. The process of checking does not compromise the structural integrity of a log in any way if engineered properly.

© 2003 David O. Marlow

Camp Marshmallow

Living area: 899 sq. ft.
Basement: none
Decks and porches: 330 sq. ft.

Bedrooms: 2
Bathrooms: 1

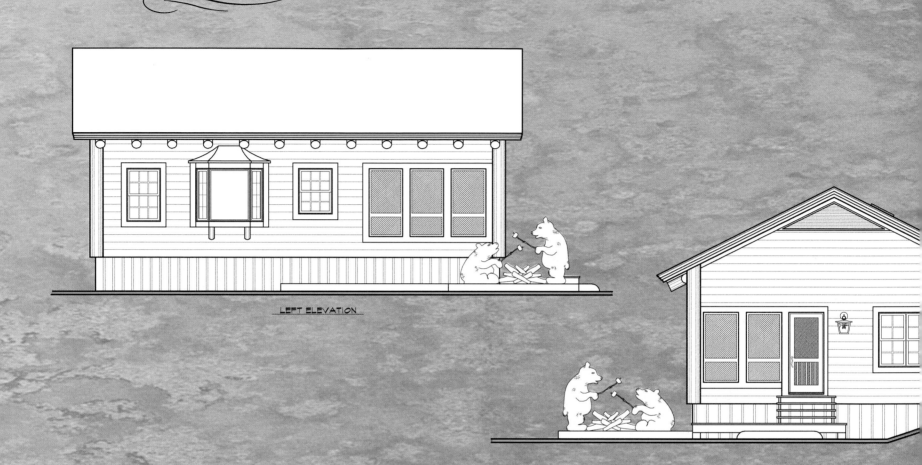

LEFT ELEVATION

Camp Marshmallow has many playful elements, incorporating bits of nature in its design. The fresh and unprocessed look of this home features a rafter roof system that feels like a touch of forest inside, with a canopy of pines overhead creating a rhythm of logs throughout the home. Outdoor living is also important in this house's plan, which includes a screened-in porch and plenty of outdoor decks.

The efficient use of limited space allows the freedom of not being held hostage by the trappings of a large home. For example, the kitchen is tucked into the home's design with the creative use of a bump-out that carves some additional space in this small home design. The second bedroom could incorporate bunk beds for added sleeping area.

A number of carefully considered details add to the charm of this home. A skylight is installed above the bathroom to create a light-filled room. A window seat has been added for additional seating space within the living room area. In the dining area, a built-in L-shaped bench allows for informal camp-style dining.

Log-Element Features

The main roof structure, built with a vaulted ceiling of log rafters, is a striking feature that makes this simple structure feel larger in size. Log railings could be added to the screened-in porch area for rustic detail.

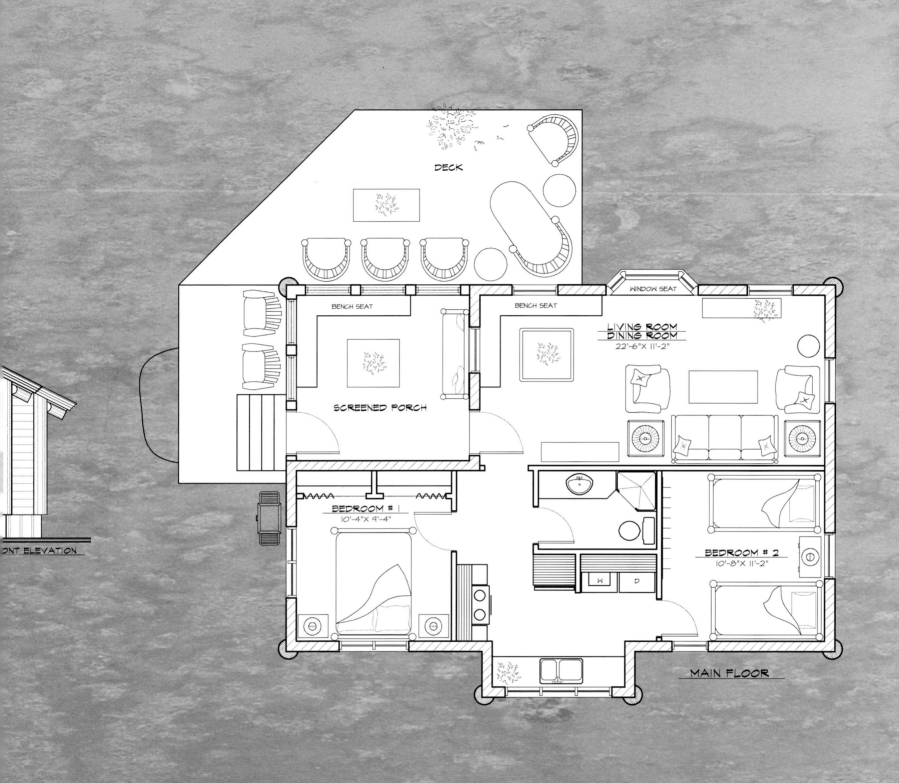

DECK

WINDOW SEAT

BENCH SEAT

BENCH SEAT

LIVING ROOM
DINING ROOM
22'-6"X 11'-2"

SCREENED PORCH

BEDROOM # 1
10'-4"X 9'-4"

BEDROOM # 2
10'-8"X 11'-2"

W   D

FRONT ELEVATION

MAIN FLOOR

The gazebo-style dining nook has a canopy of large logs that hover overhead. The "bank" of windows captures the great views of nature where the frames are trimmed with hand-hewn log slabs.

Log elements accent these two simple four-corner, conventionally framed camps. The rental camps, when completed, will overlook Lake George in the Adirondacks. Each structure needed to be limited to a 26 x 32-foot foundation and remain cost-efficient. Both camps pack a lot of design punch and appear much larger than the design suggests. Two very different designs were accomplished within the very same outside footprint.

Accents of log elements fill this home, from the twig dining table, coffee table, and chairs, to architectural elements such as the bark left on the log mantel, to the log posts that support a gazebo-style roof system. The beautifully and painstakingly hammered metal leaf pattern and bear form this handcrafted fireplace screen. These finishing touches help bring a log-element home to life.

Dream Weaver

Living area: 2,167 sq. ft.
Basement with apartment: 1,232 sq. ft.
Decks and porches: 1,688 sq. ft.

Bedrooms: 4
Bathrooms: 3

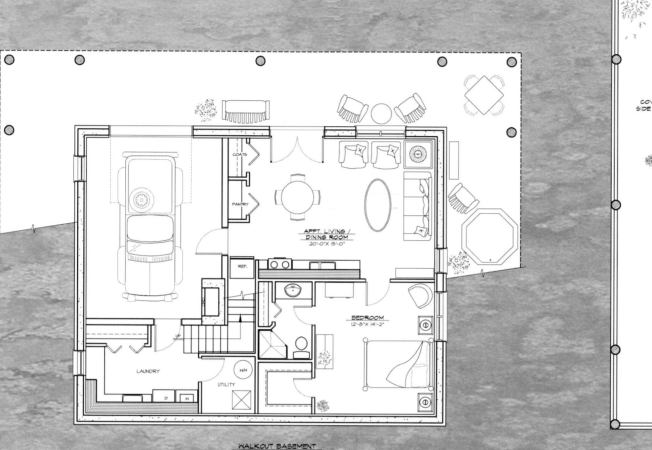

WALKOUT BASEMENT

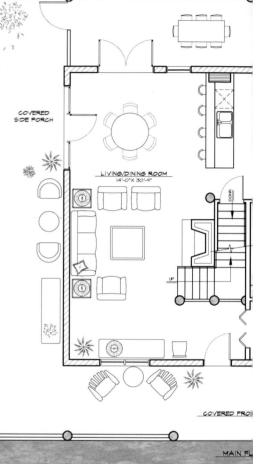

MAIN FL

In the Dream Weaver plan, the public areas flow in and out of each other, with a kitchen that includes an oversized pantry for all those extra cabin provisions. The first floor has two bedrooms and a shared bath. The second floor has a master suite that provides a private getaway, with a bathroom carved out of a central dormer. There is also a small loft that has the feel of an eagle's nest perched above the living room.

There is a triple bonus in the walkout basement — it incorporates a garage, laundry room, and a private full apartment suite for family and friends.

But the highlight of the house is its wraparound porch, which offers many seating and dining areas to enjoy the outdoor views, extending the home's living space.

Log-Element Features

The porch's roof system incorporates log rafters that march in rhythm above your head. An artful eclectic mix of Adirondack twig art is free-formed into an entry peak that pulls one in. Free-form twig sculpture is placed throughout the porch railing system, adding a touch of the Adirondack rusticity.

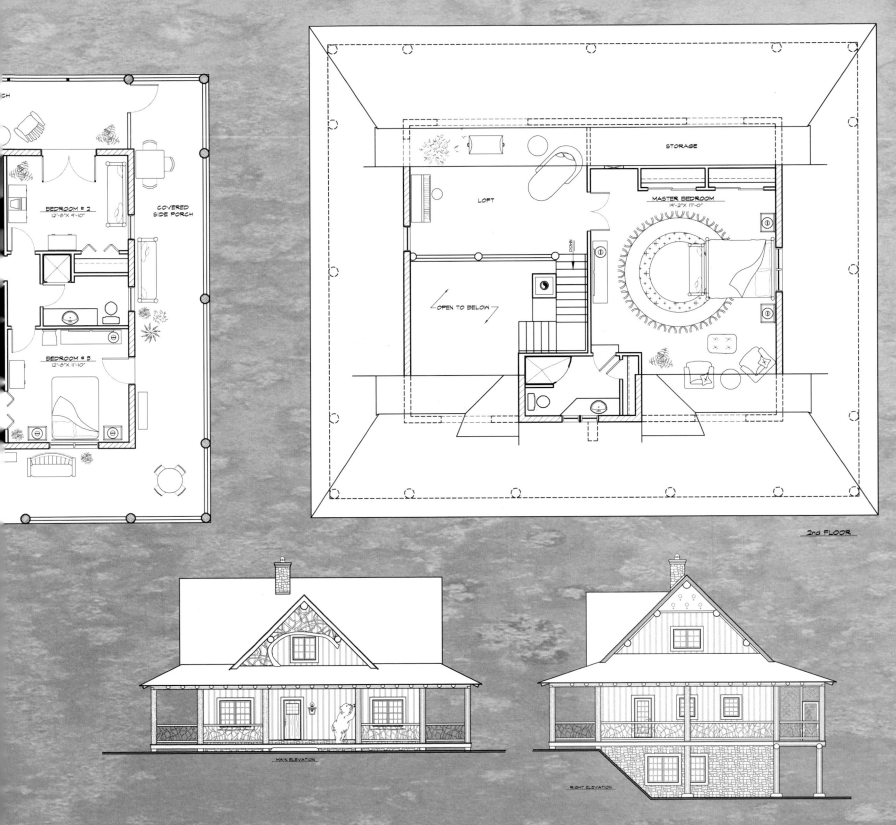

BEDROOM # 2
12'-8"X 9'-10"

COVERED
SIDE PORCH

BEDROOM # 3
12'-8"X 11'-10"

STORAGE

LOFT

MASTER BEDROOM
19'-2"X 17'-0"

DOWN

OPEN TO BELOW

2nd FLOOR

MAIN ELEVATION

RIGHT ELEVATION

Taking Cues from **NATURE** */ 105*

This Adirondack camp incorporates log rafters that run from the roof ridge down to cover and pass over the top of the exterior walls. The base cord log is called a tie beam, or collar tie, and is not only a decorative element but also a very important structural component that keeps the constant "thrust" of the roof rafters that can spread the top of the walls over time.

The Adirondack design flair is classic and timeless and is no longer limited to the Adirondacks. Adirondack design can be seen in California, Colorado, Georgia, New Hampshire, and Maine, among other places. This style is also a very popular influence in the Great Lakes cabin-and-cottage country of Wisconsin and Minnesota.

The overhead ceiling uses a triple log girder as support because of the smaller-diameter logs that need to span the large opening. The hand-built birch-bark canoe hangs from the ceiling as a work of art, boasting its beautiful hand-split cedar ribs and spruce roots that tie the canoe's side rails. This home's dark green walls contrast the soft white birch-bark bookshelf.

Large-diameter hand-hewn ceiling joists are a traditional timber-frame element. Antler lighting fixtures and Mission-style furniture mixed with twig-art end tables and junkyard finds give this Adirondack camp a great design.

Pine Hill Bluff

Living area: 1,563 sq. ft.
Basement: 780 sq. ft.
Decks and porches: 396 sq. ft.

Bedrooms: 4
Bathrooms: 2 plus outdoor shower

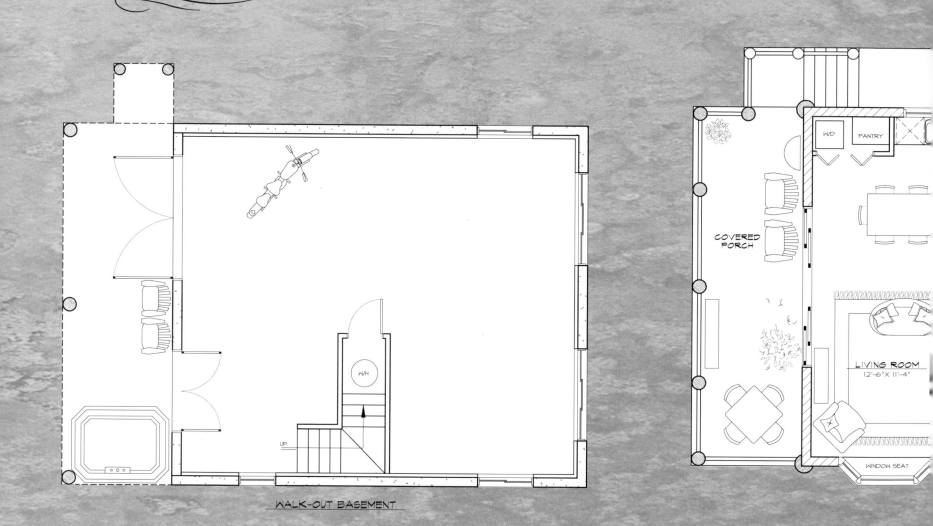

WALK-OUT BASEMENT

Pine Hill Bluff is reminiscent of a New England–style barn. Simplicity and comfort for family, guests, and friends characterize this open floor plan.

The cupola on top allows for great aesthetics as well as provides a practical but brilliant rooftop vent. The vent creates a natural air-conducting system that, when opened in the summer, creates a "chimney effect" of cool air that sweeps through the home. A multitude of windows floods this home with light, with built-in bay windows to extend the seating area.

An outdoor shower is the perfect place for a hot summer rinse, and is private and comfortable enough to be in great demand. Inside, a ladder to the observatory loft adds to the home's sense of style. A walkout basement is incorporated into the plan for possible future expansion.

Log-Element Features

The covered porch area has exposed log ceiling joists. There are log rails in the porch, stairs, and loft area, creating a complex rhythm of log work throughout the home.

The main roof system is made up of log purlins with hidden supports built into the exterior walls and exposed log columns through the home's center. Ceiling joists are used as decorative log elements throughout the main floor's ceilings while supporting the floor system above.

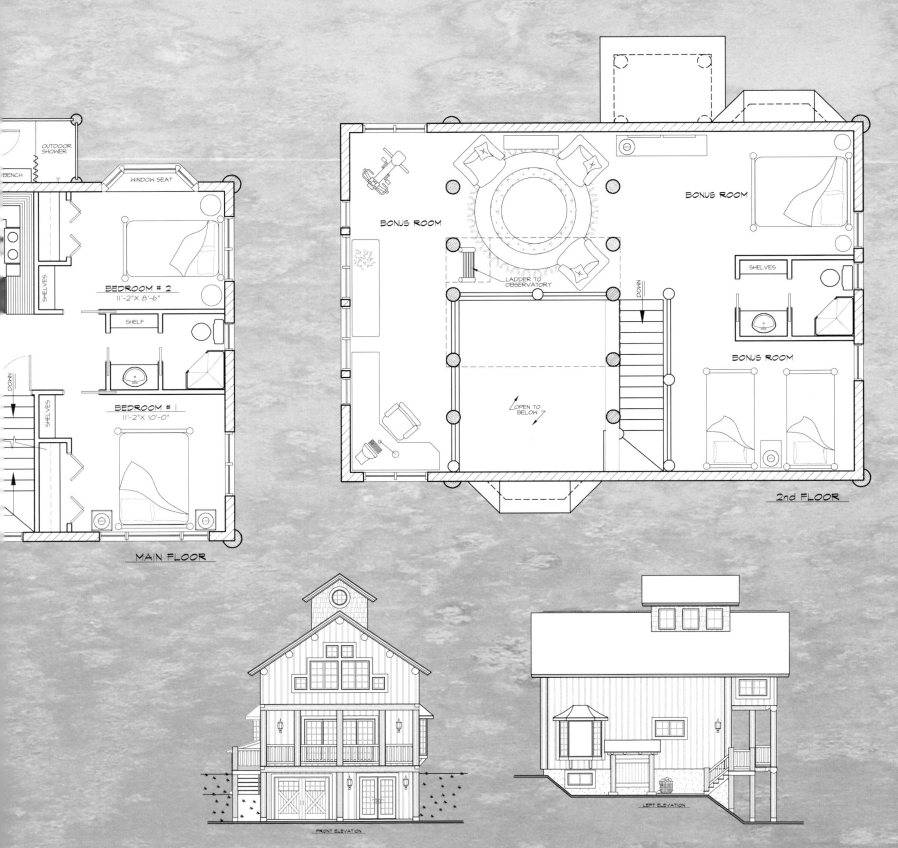

OUTDOOR
SHOWER

BENCH

WINDOW SEAT

SHELVES

BEDROOM # 2
11'-2"X 8'-6"

SHELF

DOWN

SHELVES

BEDROOM # 1
11'-2"X 10'-0"

MAIN FLOOR

BONUS ROOM

LADDER TO
OBSERVATORY

DOWN

OPEN TO
BELOW

BONUS ROOM

SHELVES

BONUS ROOM

2nd FLOOR

FRONT ELEVATION

LEFT ELEVATION

Taking Cues from **NATURE** / 109

The twig art of the Adirondacks comes in many forms. Craftspeople are limited only by their imaginations and ingenuity. Talented twig artist Rita Dee has transformed the Hudson River's driftwood into a work of art. Dee also designed Pine Hill Bluff.

© 2003 Andy Wainwright

Trout House

Living area: 997 sq. ft.
Basement apartment: 704 sq. ft.
Decks and porches: 450 sq. ft.

Bedrooms: 2
Bathrooms: 3

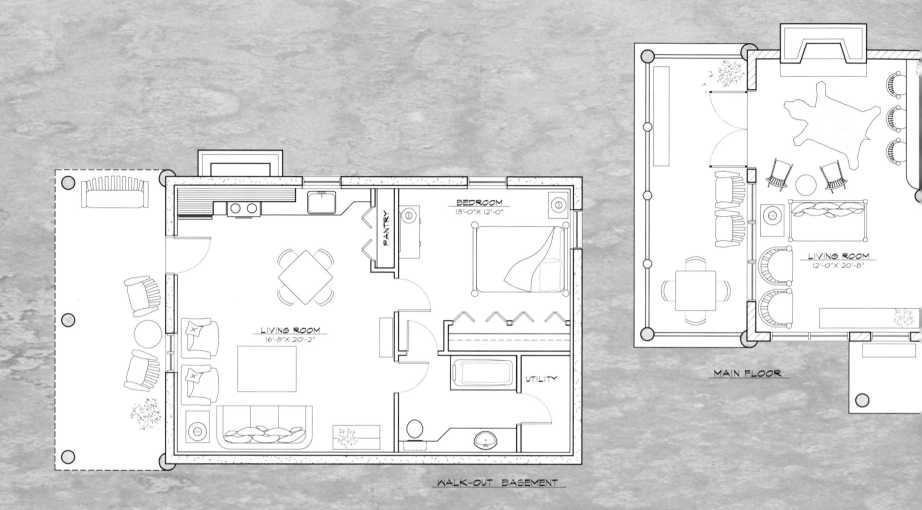

LIVING ROOM 16'-8"X 20'-2"

PANTRY

BEDROOM 13'-0"X 12'-0"

UTILITY

WALK-OUT BASEMENT

LIVING ROOM 12'-0"X 20'-8"

MAIN FLOOR

The conservative footprint of Trout House seems to swell beyond its dimensions with its open floor plan. The free-flowing space of this home makes a great vacation home or wonderful retirement retreat. Several covered porches and decks add plenty of room for outdoor fun and relaxation.

The main floor incorporates an oversized fireplace. A covered wood storage bin is conveniently located near the front door for easy access to the fireplace. There are two large bathrooms, both with a hot tub and shower. The loft tucked above has spectacular views through the expansive plate of windows over the living room area that takes in the natural surroundings. The bonus walkout basement has a one-bedroom guest suite that is private and self-sufficient.

Log-Element Features

An artful scissors truss is a beautiful focal point above the main entry door. The main roof system is an elaborate mix of large log trusses, purlins, and ridgepoles. Log railings are incorporated into the covered porch, the balcony, and the second-floor bedroom loft area.

Part of the second-floor loft system is supported by log floor joists and a center log girder. The other half of the floor system is built of conventional materials, and houses the structure's mechanical systems. The second-floor bathroom has log purlins and ridgepoles that create additional headroom and interest in the bathroom area.

OPEN TO BELOW

LOFT
12'-0"X 20'-8"

W/D

STORAGE
UNDER STAIRS

UP

2nd FLOOR

LEFT ELEVATION

ENTRY ELEVATION

BACK ELEVATION

For the Trout House's covered porch, the owner asked for furniture to be made out of the leftover scraps from the building of the two rental camps. The stools and base of the table are made of the stumps of the log ends or cutoffs of truss and purlin members. The tabletop was made out of a large-diameter log slab. The look is casual yet very durable for the onslaught of vacationers that stay at this new log-element Adirondack camp.

© 2003 Beaver Creek Log Homes

The garden archway frames the entry of the gate leading to the fenced-in back yard. A naturally arched cedar log sapling is used to create the arch. The use of winter-cut materials helps retain the natural bark of the log, making the bark a more secure addition to the log for years of use.

© 2003 Robbin Obomsawin
Artist: Ugene Slade

Furnishings can play off the architectural components of a log-element home, as in this cabin, where the smaller scale of twig-art furnishings with their natural dark bark contrasts with the oversized scale of naturally light log elements.

© 2003 Rob Melnychuk

Chapter Five

Log Elegance

Today's log homes often reflect a level of luxury that couldn't have been imagined by the early pioneers who built the first log cabins in the United States. Homeowners today desire the amenities of modern living combined with the natural beauty of logs, and this combination is reflected in the homes that make up this section.

Some characteristics that many of these homes share include cathedral ceilings, sweeping great rooms, and cozy lofts bordered by log railings.

The combination of skip-peeled logs and an experienced log builder and design professional creates a home with many log elements that provides a feeling of being wrapped in trees.

Bear Mountain Lodge

Living area: 1,864 sq. ft.
Basement: 1,224 sq. ft.
Decks and porches: 846 sq. ft.

Bedrooms: 3
Bathrooms: 3

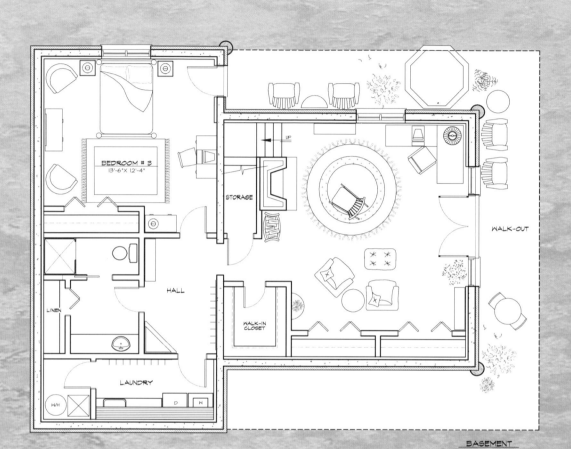

BASEMENT

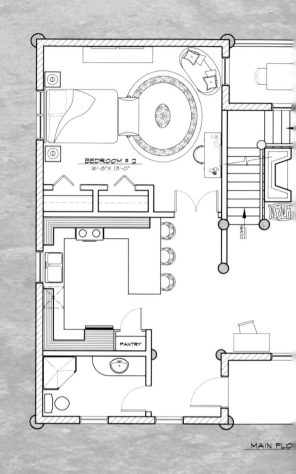

MAIN FLO

The plan for Bear Mountain Lodge has a casual but elegant feel. This home's layout is perfect for a sloping property with a view. The wraparound porch allows for plenty of outdoor living space and affords many spots to enjoy the outdoor views.

Inside, fireplaces are the focal points of the main floor and basement living areas. The kitchen's wraparound style is efficient and spacious, with an effective work triangle built into its design. The main floor bedroom could alternatively be made into a more formal dining area. Upstairs, the second-floor loft has a master bedroom suite with a private sitting room/den.

The walkout basement has plenty of room and is versatile. It could be used as a kids' retreat, a suite for guests, or a great in-home office with its own private entrance.

Log-Element Features

The sculptural form of this home is breathtaking. Its intersecting rooflines are poetry with a canopy of logs overhead. The covered porch roof system is equipped to house lighting and outdoor speaker systems. Log timbers flank the entry into the informal living room/dining area. The arrowhead railings, made of the most modest materials, create an open fretwork pattern and give the home extra character. Standard log railings enclose the area around the stairs and loft.

The main floor's ceiling system is an intersection of log floor joists and log girders, which become supports for the second floor above. The large log timbers sweep dramatically across the main floor's ceilings. The second-floor roof system is constructed of log purlins with a few log dormers that carve out space for a great master bathroom.

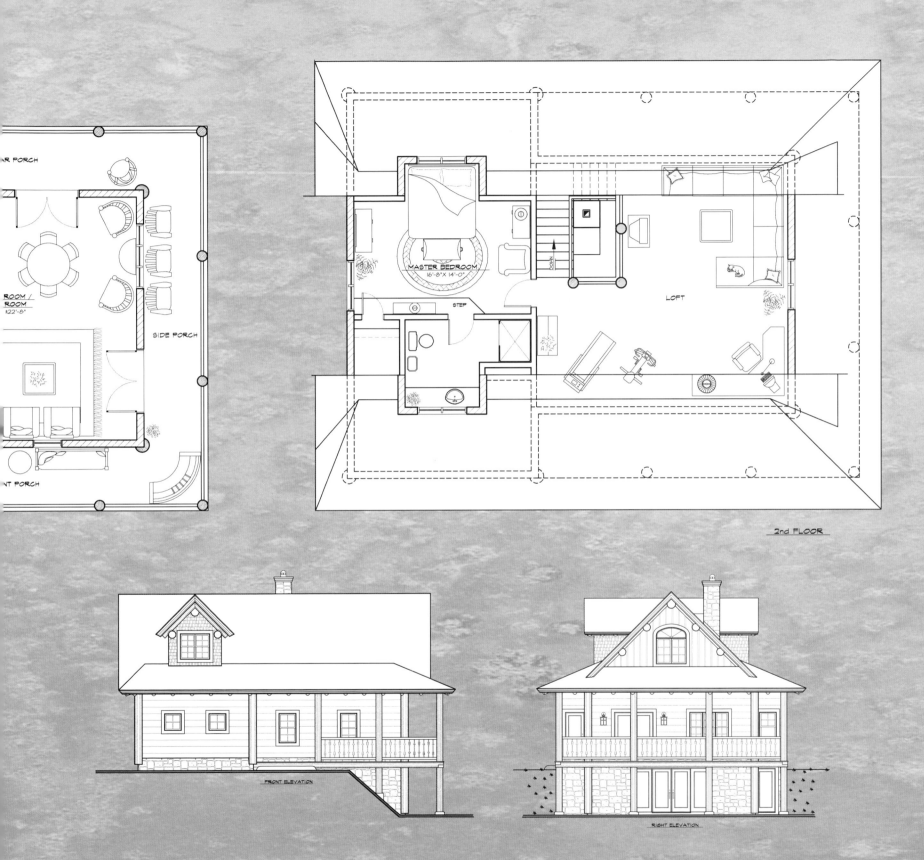

AR PORCH

ROOM /
ROOM
±22'-8"

SIDE PORCH

NT PORCH

MASTER BEDROOM
16'-8"X 14'-0"

STEP

LOFT

2nd FLOOR

FRONT ELEVATION

RIGHT ELEVATION

This bathroom has a tub and a view fit for a king or queen. The low-pitched roof and short king post over the tub carry the long lengths of purlins and ridgepoles above.

© 2003 Roger Wade

Vibrant colors, natural materials, and rounded stucco curves give this kitchen a southwestern flavor. The gazebo-style bump-out with a fan of log work supported by a forked log post draws your eyes to the intersection of logs above. The striking feature of the curved window captures a panoramic view, creating a kitchen to live in.

© 2003 Roger Wade

Eagle's Dance

Living area: 2,522 sq. ft.
Basement: none
Decks and porches: 619 sq. ft.

Bedrooms: 3
Bathrooms: 3

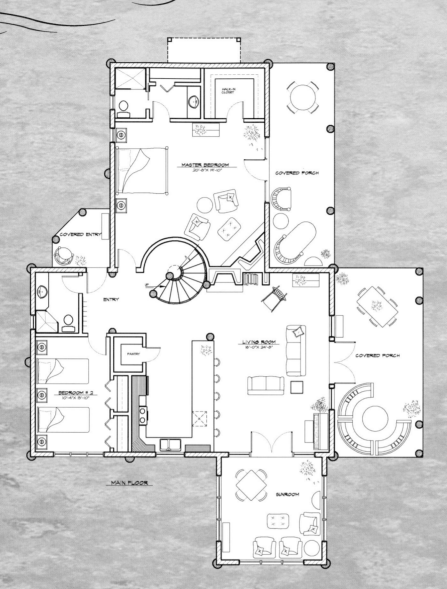

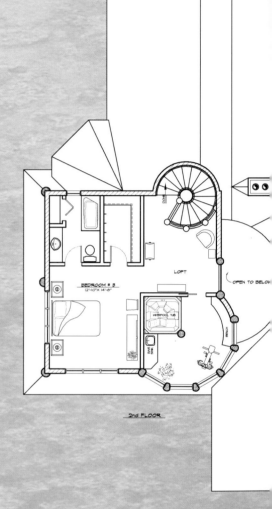

The irresistible look and style of this sprawling home is topped with a master suite and tower room. A second oversized master suite with large bathrooms and walk-in closets is located on the main floor.

In the living area, an oversized double fireplace warms this home's soul. The light-filled sunroom could be used as a formal dining room, billiard room, or casual living/dining area.

The home's exterior has a sculptural form whose fluid movement is interesting from all four angles. Its asymmetrical design emphasizes a connection with nature, and the many windows incorporated into the design create a dance of light throughout the day. There are several covered porches, designed to maximize outdoor relaxation and fun.

Log-Element Features

The cathedral log roof systems in the main master suite, living room, and sunroom offer drama as the varying ceiling lights create visual interest. A set of log spiral stairs sweeps up to the second-floor master suite and loft. A balcony-style loft with log railings overlooks the living room below, while the second-floor master loft incorporates log ceiling joists.

RIGHT ELEVATION

LEFT ELEVATION

BACK ELEVATION

A striking contrast is achieved by the use of log elements
with chink-style methods and a stucco finish. Doubled log
purlins add visual interest and support snow loads.

© 2003 Rocky Mountain Log Homes

The massive log fireplace
mantel, ceiling, floor joists,
and log stairs produce
warmth and texture in the
basement living area.

© 2003 Rocky Mountain Log Homes

The design professional for this home made timber-frame trusses with a split king post, then
used a decorative trough-rod connection in the
form of a star. The log elements of trusses,
square purlins, and log-element stools provide a
casual contrast to the more formal kitchen décor.

© 2003 David O. Marlow

Red Canyon Lodge

Living area: 2,749 sq. ft.
Basement: none
Decks and porches: 856 sq. ft.

Bedrooms: 3
Bathrooms: 2

FRONT ELEVATION

The T-shaped log-element structure has visual interest no matter from which angle it is viewed. Dramatic log elements are seamlessly integrated into the home's design with well-thought-out proportions. The starburst board patterns provide a playful element adding a designer flair to this home. The exterior balconies and porches create a home with a lot of usable outdoor living space.

The cabin's entry is spacious and grand, with the added convenience of an attached garage for easy access to the main living area. The kitchen is large, configured in a wraparound layout that incorporates a large walk-in pantry, perfect for the gourmet cook who is armed with a collection of kitchenware. A grand set of stairs sweeps up to a comfortable landing. Both bedrooms on the second floor have private balconies designed for flexible use. The second-floor bathroom is large with a wraparound vanity. The room is large enough for both an oversized shower and a soaking tub.

Log-Element Features

This design is loaded with log detail, with covered porches and balconies that incorporate log trusses and columns in the railing systems. Log planters are attached to the home's exterior, adding drama to the windows' height.

The main floor system is a combination of log trusses and purlins that intersect a secondary set of bump-out purlins, providing the dormer that houses the bathroom. The ceiling joists of the main floor are rustic logs that support the second-floor system.

COVERED PORCH

WALK-IN
CLOSET

MASTER BEDROOM
16'-4" X 13'-4"

PANTRY

ENTRY

MAIN FLOOR

DINING ROOM
LIVING ROOM
26'-6" X 13'-6"

COVERED PORCH

LEFT ELEVATION

COVERED BALCONY

BEDROOM # 2
20'-4" X 13'-4"

DOWN

BEDROOM # 3
16'-6" X 11'-4"

COVERED BALCONY

2nd FLOOR

Who says that basements are dark, damp, and dingy? Quality interior design can break the mold of a typical basement. Here, the basement footprint allows a pleasing and comfortable living area for family and friends. Incorporating log elements into the basement adds interest and continuity to the home's overall design. Stonework and added niches (one of which encloses a kitchenette) all enhance the log elements that add mass and substance to this conventionally built structure.

© 2003 Rocky Mountain Log Homes

This home has textured walls with sculptural form that is highlighted with a mix of log elements. The raised dining area is guarded by a set of log railings. Oversized log slabs are used successfully with the outer natural shape of the logs (called the wanes of the board or log), left unmilled for an artful flair. The log artisans worked with all the natural imperfections of the whole logs by using the crooks of the logs as part of the art of the design. The log rails bow and curve, while the spindles of the railings are left with its natural bumps, and part of the logs' inner barks (called cambium) were left unpolished. Also note how the light-colored wall surfaces contrast nicely with the darker wood ceilings, creating a sculptural form as the slope of the roof meets the walls.

© 2003 Roger Wade

Whistler's Notch

Living area: 2,080 sq. ft.
Basement: 1,248 sq. ft.
Decks and porches: 279 sq. ft.

Bedrooms: 3
Bathrooms: 3

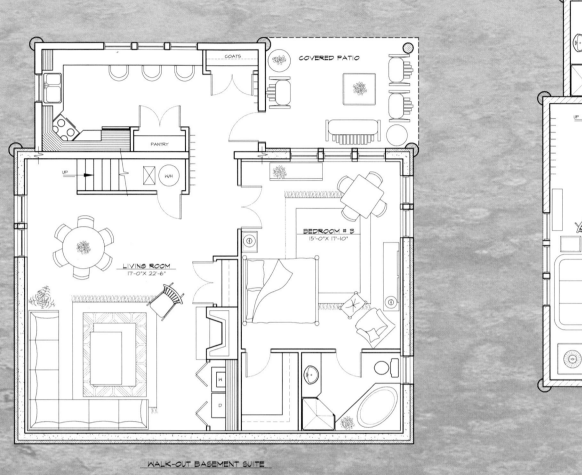

WALK-OUT BASEMENT SUITE

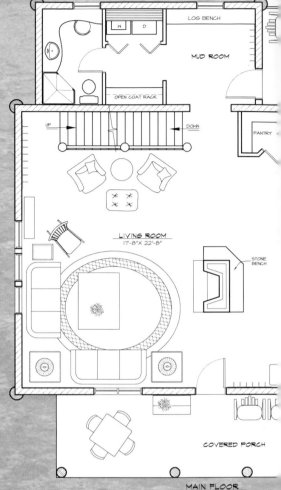

MAIN FLOOR

Whistler's Notch at first appears to be a small traditional cottage in the woods, but, as seen from the back, it is actually three times the size of its first impression. Large English-cottage–style windows usher in the light. The second-floor gable-end windows have an "eye-brow" transom panel above with a sunburst pattern of boards that accentuate a standard window. The home incorporates many covered porch areas.

The main floor is an open free-flowing space. A centrally located fireplace can be made extra-efficient as a Russian stove or masonry fire unit. The mudroom/laundry room has log rafters above that create a beautiful roof system. The second-floor hallway is a light-filled space and architecturally interesting landing.

A bonus area in the walkout basement has a large and luxurious apartment. Wraparound windows in the basement's kitchen and bedroom create a sunroom feel.

Log-Element Features

The entry porch has log rafters that march down the length of the home. The open floor allows a view of the first floor's ceiling system of log joists that support the floor above. The second-floor roof system is made up of log posts and purlins as well as a row of log rafters within the large shed dormer.

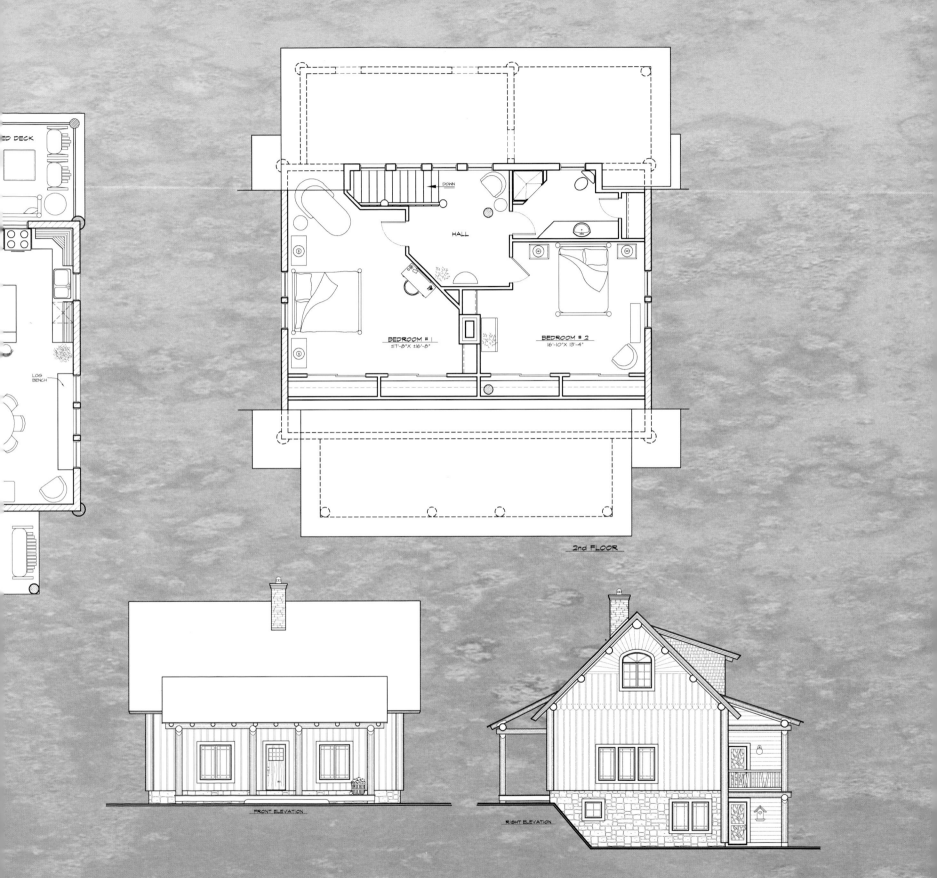

ED DECK

LOG
BENCH

DOWN

HALL

BEDROOM # 1
±17'-8" X ±16'-8"

BEDROOM # 2
16'-10" X 13'-4"

2nd FLOOR

FRONT ELEVATION

RIGHT ELEVATION

The large-diameter timber-frame trusses are a focal point of this great room. The mix of the smooth surface of the plaster walls, stone columns, and fireplace hearth provide a great textural contrast, giving the room more depth and interest. An Arts & Crafts—style mantel's header tops the fireplace alcove with a gracefully sweeping design.

All © 2003 Charles Cunniffe Architects

This contemporary home has a touch of rustic casual elegance. The heavy squared timbers are designed with a Craftsman style of joinery, with iron straps that not only work as structural components but also become works of art with their detail and proportions.

The "lucky dog" welcomes us to the gates of this grand entry. A large timber-frame truss caps the stone columns and oversized doors, blending with this home's architectural details, those of a contemporary Arts & Crafts—style log-element structure.

A log-element pass-through peers into the gourmet kitchen. The honed granite counters radiate a natural, low-luster finish against the log work. The stone countertop is mortised into the log column for a true Craftsman finish.

© 2003 Charles Cunniffe Architects

The kitchen is the dream of a gourmet cook, with a commercial-style range surrounded by a stone hearth feature. The log-element columns are designed as a pass-through, with a beautiful stained-glass transom inlaid into the log work.

© 2003 Charles Cunniffe Architects

The scribed and mitered connecting points of the home's log-element trusses become this home's focal point. Skip-peeled logs retain the inner layer of the bark, producing a rustic style without being pressure-washed off. This type of skip-peeled effect is only possible under a certain combination of conditions.

© 2003 David O. Marlow

This kitchen is conventionally built with standard wall-framed systems. The log elements within the roof system show beautifully executed craftsmanship. The overall balance of architecture, design, and handcrafted log work is harmonious. The combinations of textures and color create plenty of visual interest.

© 2003 Roger Wade

Chapter Six

Outbuildings & Small Spaces

O n the opposite end of the scale, some crave the intimacy that only small spaces can provide. And what better way to create intimacy than with the warmth of logs? Incorporating log elements into small homes and apartments or garages and other outbuildings can add a touch of nature to any surrounding. The examples here are simple structures enhanced with log elements.

The bumps and jogs of this home's design create dramatic rooflines, carving out a special place for a set of louver-style beds. The room's backdrop has a painting of a lakeside seen as if viewed from the mountaintop.

© 2003 Roger Wade

Carriage House Garage

Living area: 806 sq. ft.   Bedrooms: 1
Basement garage: 884 sq. ft.   Bathrooms: 1
Main floor garage: 884 sq. ft.

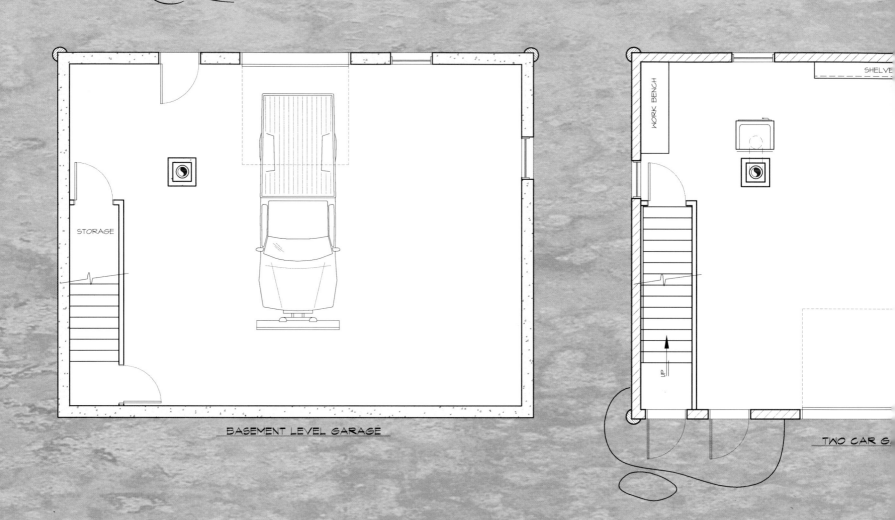

STORAGE

BASEMENT LEVEL GARAGE

WORK BENCH

SHELVE

UP

TWO CAR G.

This classic carriage house even includes a caretaker's flat. There is a two-car bay located on the main-floor level with a workbench and shelving. The woodstove is a wonderful addition to the workshop for those long, cold winter projects. Stairs lead to another lower-level garage, which takes advantage of a hillside slope that daylights the garage for added storage of boats, recreational vehicles, snowplows, and heavy equipment, as well as gardening and yard equipment; it can also be modified to suit other needs.

The separate entry door climbs to the upper-level apartment, which also has the added warmth of a central woodstove. The living area feels open and spacious. The dine-in kitchen is carved out of the roof system by incorporating a log rafter dormer. The bar-style kitchen has a refrigerator tucked under the counter, along with plenty of additional storage in a walk-in pantry.

The bedroom suite has a large walk-in closet and a good-sized bathroom with a tub tucked under the slope of the roofline meeting the knee wall. The conventionally built three-story structure has character no matter what angle it is viewed from. The carved crowing rooster is the crowning touch that sings, no matter what the time of day.

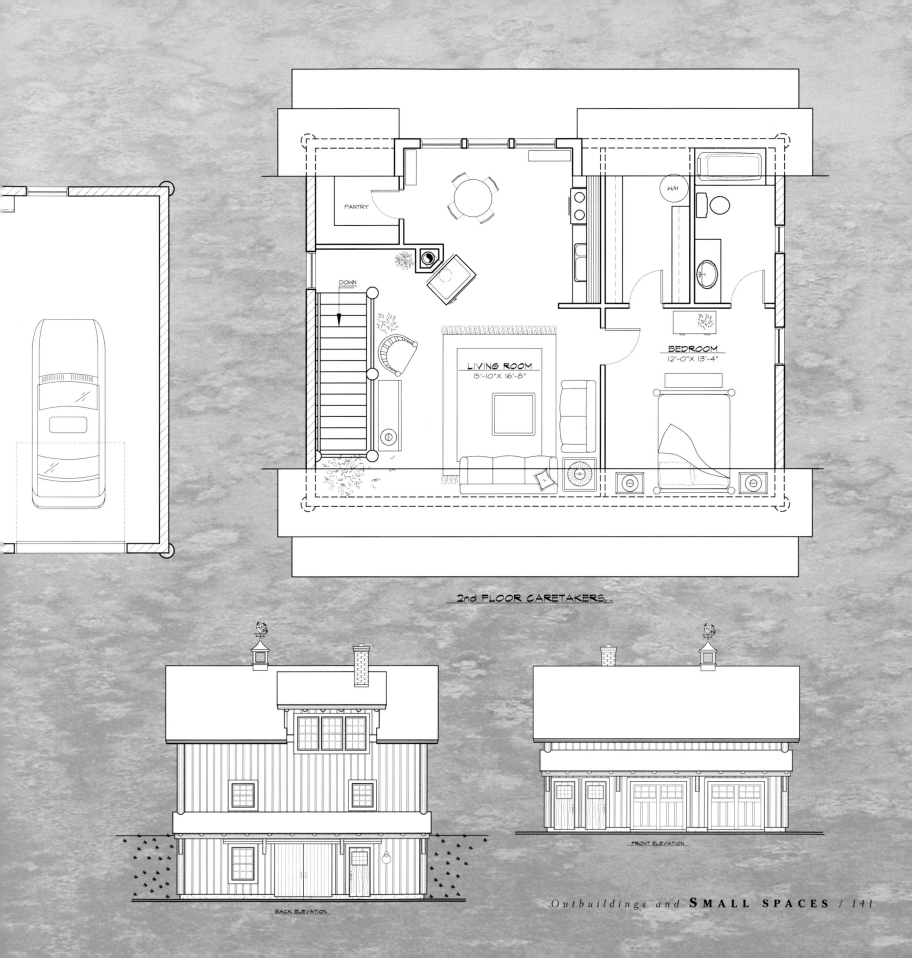

PANTRY

DOWN

W/H

LIVING ROOM
15'-10" X 16'-8"

BEDROOM
12'-0" X 13'-4"

2nd FLOOR CARETAKERS.

BACK ELEVATION

FRONT ELEVATION

This lakeside boat house was built with a weekend apartment on top. The log elements, such as the twig art and tree forms that flank the stairs and frame the balcony, seem to have grown out of the lake. They are simple and subtle, but pack a punch in architectural interest.

© 2003 Robbin Obomsawin

Saltbox Garage

Living area: 484 sq. ft.

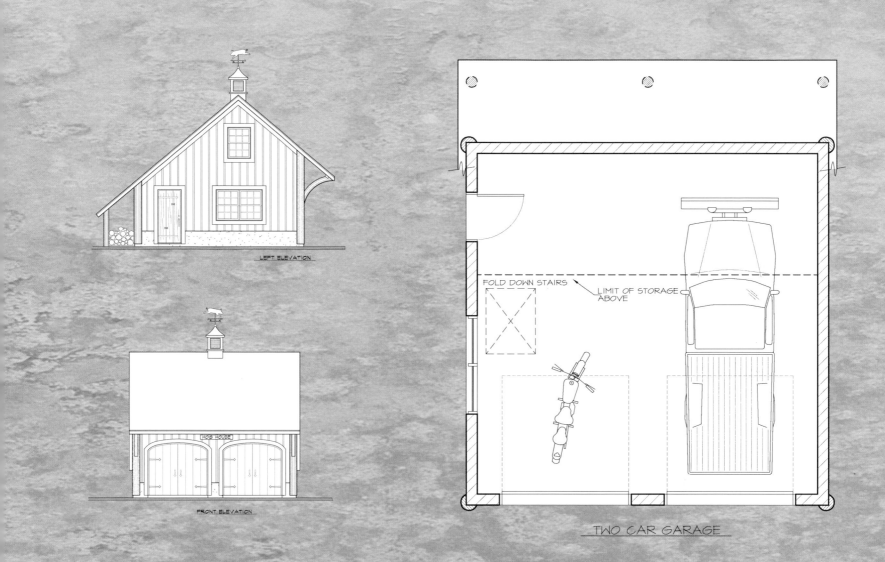

LEFT ELEVATION

HOG HOUSE

FRONT ELEVATION

FOLD DOWN STAIRS

LIMIT OF STORAGE ABOVE

TWO CAR GARAGE

This New England saltbox roofline has a classic shape. The two-car bay is perfect for additional storage of garden tools, lawn equipment, and boat storage, or is the perfect cover for the Harley as a comfortable "hog" house (which fits right in with the flying pig weather vane).

The side door allows quick access. Inside there is a pull-down ladder to a small attic storage area. The extended roofline creates a great area for wood storage. The garage doors can be attached with hinges like a traditional garage or barn door, or the garage can be modified and adapted to become a one-door unit in combination with an electrical garage-door opener. This design is most requested by clients who prefer to have an alternative area in which to retreat.

Two–Bay Garage

Living area: 780 sq. ft.

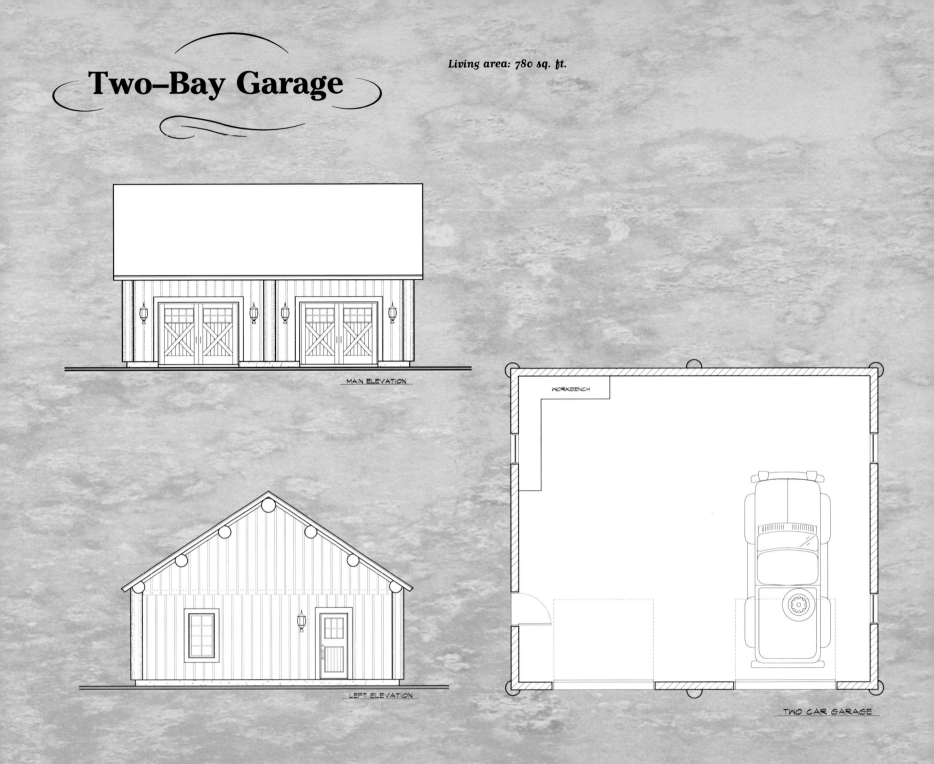

MAIN ELEVATION

LEFT ELEVATION

WORKBENCH

TWO CAR GARAGE

This two-bay garage is a classic board-and-batten style–garage with "cap" logs on the exterior corners. The design of the garage doors exudes a sense of tradition. The log purlins are not only decorative, but help to tie the garage to the log-element home you choose. This is a simple cost-effective garage to build.

Three–Bay Garage

Living area: 962 sq. ft.

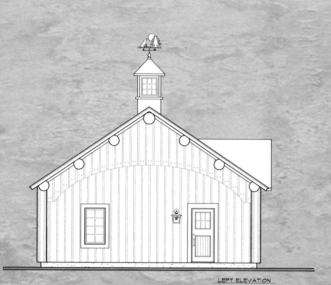

LEFT ELEVATION

MAIN ELEVATION

This classic three-bay garage is charming and elegant. Its traditionally built doors are a perfect detail that enhances the structure's design. The center bay has a log ridgepole and purlins to add architectural interest and symmetry to the building. Decorative purlins on the gable create interest and texture. The artful cupola tops the roof, with a weather vane as an accent.

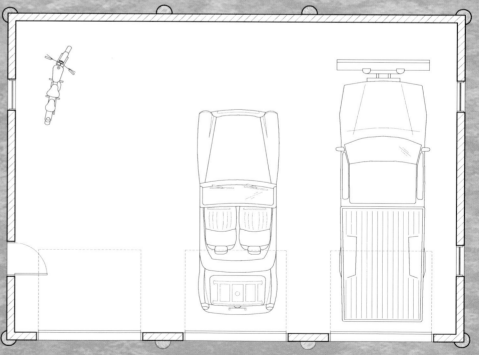

THREE CAR GARAGE

The slope of a second-floor loft can limit the amount of headroom. With smart placement of furniture, you can make better use of this space. There is something magical about a loft—kind of a tree house charm or eagle's nest in the sky.

© 2003 Roger Wade

This bunkhouse also doubles as a lakeside dock. The bunkhouse is very small but has served as a guestroom for many years with only a full-sized double bunk and dressers. The structure, built into the hillside, was built with conventional methods. The roof system, columns, and rails are constructed of winter-cut red cedar, chosen for its ability to retain its textural bark. Built in the 1930s, this structure still stands the test of time.

© 2003 Robbin Obomsawin

The log-element style of a gazebo room is used in the dining room's panoramic viewing area. The natural twists and free-form spirals of juniper wood on the table and chairs, used in combination with rawhide laced-back chairs, add a touch of whimsy. The log rafters are beautiful structural elements that create a rhythmic dome of logs overhead.

© 2003 Roger Wade

The use of bold fabrics and painted furniture adds vibrancy to a room in which a telescope is not needed to find the stars.

© 2003 Rocky Mountain Log Homes

Epilogue

Building for a Lifetime

A log-element structure is selected for its uniqueness, sculptural form, function, and high quality of workmanship. It is here where utility and art mesh—not just through décor but as a way of life where everything is considered. This architectural form blurs the line between what is man-made and what is natural.

The enjoyment of designing and building a custom home is not found just in the completed project. The journey of design and the process of building can also bring great satisfaction. By understanding our goals and project parameters, we create a home design with energy that goes beyond the four walls to capture the experience of nature, our surroundings, and our love of life.

G CABIN · THE NOT SO LOG CABIN · THE NOT

All of us are reflections of our past habits, interests, and experiences in life. As we analyze our needs, we will discover the ways to obtain the most from our home design, ways that demonstrate the care and sensitivity we put into it. A log-element structure is selected for its uniqueness, sculptural form, function, and high quality of workmanship. It is here where utility and art mesh — not just through décor but as a way of life where everything is considered. This architectural form blurs the line between what is man-made and what is natural.

With careful thought and consideration we can make our home a healthy house or a "green building" with the specifications incorporated into our designs. We could leave a legacy of architecture devoted to natural materials, classic designs, and fine craftsmanship, transcending all other styles that come and go.

To wrap oneself in nature is healing, but we must learn to give more than we take and value the environment that surrounds us. We will not only minimize damage to our property, but as we respect the home design and building site so that it becomes one with its surroundings, it will provide timeless classic quality and beauty for generations to treasure.

Each piece of property has its own poetry. Making the home a natural part of this rhythm takes extra sensitive attention. Once one has learned to respect nature, the spirit of the dance of life is captured.

We are only a small part of this large world and ought to have respect for the overwhelming power of Mother Nature. We can easily be in sync with nature and not fight against or try to "improve" her artistry. As we learn to embrace simplicity, we often find that things we have always felt were important may turn out to be insignificant and unnecessary.

If we stand quietly in the midst of nature, we can feel the humbling power of its force. Our eyes will be opened to see the world in a different way. Natural building materials produce a healthy, comfortable living environment not only for you and your family, but also for our world and future generations. Building without an understanding of how "disposable" housing affects our future is irresponsible. We are accountable for the choices we make every day for the world we share.

Reclaimed hand-hewn timbers are worked into this new home's design, with log columns, corbels, and squared log floor joists that create a U-shaped loft above. Note the use of inlaid recycled floorboards that have been mitered at their intersecting points, becoming a frame for the large handcrafted tiles.

© 2003 Conklin's Authentic Antique Barnwood

Working with Contractors

Your project is only as good as your general contractor, who will serve as the team leader. A good general contractor will know how to choose and manage his team well, knowing each sub-trade's expertise and which trade best fits the required task. Builders work under rough site conditions and tight construction deadlines, and must coordinate with many other tradespeople. A contractor must be flexible and compatible with all involved and must clearly understand the sub-trades' scope of work, abilities, and limitations.

Remember, the general contractor's job is stressful and can be very demanding. The contractor has to translate and incorporate the client's vision and ideas into a home, while weighing what is realistic, cost-effective, and practical for each situation. Codes vary from place to place and are continually updated. New technologies are constantly being developed or modified. A good contractor thinks ten steps ahead and three behind to make a project succeed, and is always aware of the whole picture — not just bits and pieces. The contractor is continually trying to make everyone happy — the owner, architect, lender, and building inspector. The reality of construction is that there is an ongoing battle of compromises and changes. The honeymoon is often over after a few months, once the energy and initial excitement of a new project wear thin. Worn personalities can flair on all sides and everyone begins to feel the strain, especially if the project runs over the estimated time lines or projected budget.

To protect yourself from questionable contractors, ask for references from the contractor's last ten projects. Be sure to call all the references; just one or two is not going to give you an accurate picture. Keep in mind that even though some people may say negative things about a contractor, it may or may not be a legitimate concern. It may very well be that the client is very green in the construction world or just a chronic complainer who wanted more than they paid for. Ask these people about specific problems they encountered and how the builder addressed these issues. Talk to your local building code inspector to see if they have noticed questionable or shortcut building methods with a particular builder. Do not sweep all negative comments under the rug because you are desperate for a contractor and tired of interviewing; you should not live in denial when red flags start to go up. On the other hand, if eight of the ten references are very satisfied with a particular contractor, that is a good sign that your potential contractor is dependable and can do the job the way that you envision.

Once you have chosen and hired a contractor, you must have confidence in his judgment. To second-guess every decision made by the chosen contractor or attempt to micromanage the project will undermine the entire effort. This does not mean you cannot ask questions or respectfully disagree with a decision made, but the contractor needs freedom and some leeway and trust in order to make the job run smoothly. Here are some more helpful suggestions for working smoothly with a contractor:

- Have written contracts with your general contractor, log builder, and/or project manager for the protection of all parties involved.

- Be sure your contractor does not overbook his projects or spread himself too thin so that you become a low priority. This is where references of past performances are important.

- It is expected that the general contractor will contribute to project ideas, but constant hand-holding or second-guessing the contractor and sub-trades can drastically slow down a project as well as drain the contractor. The time you spend with unnecessary questions or general chitchat is time taken away from the concentration needed on your project.

- Listen to the professional advice of your builder. Construction is not always so black and white. Practical experience over years of construction is very valuable.

- Pay contract draws and fees on time. Construction interest loans are high and materials are expensive. Contractors and sub-trades will be more likely to show up and your project will become a higher priority if they know that accounts are being paid on time.

Working with a
Third-Party Inspector

A third-party inspector is often very helpful and can bring you great peace of mind. It may be worth an additional consulting fee to have a qualified inspector, who may also be a design professional, to guide you and help sort through the information specific to your needs. The experienced inspector can also give insight into money-saving alternatives that you might not have considered in your plans. Hiring a professional for four to ten visits during critical points of the construction process can be a very cost-effective option. The third-party inspector will serve as your eyes and ears throughout critical stages of the project to ensure your home is built to code and that specifications have been met. Some of the most common services that a third-party inspector can provide are the following:

- to review plans;

- to review construction bids;

- to visit the log builder's yard to inspect the quality of joinery and materials selection before a log builder is hired;

- to visit during mid-point of foundation pour or to check for sight drainage and soil conditions;

- to pick up details that easily can be missed in joinery and structural properties as the walls are framed;

- to monitor the plumbing, electrical, and mechanical systems as they are in route; and

- to be sure the details are achieved and the punch list is completed as the finish work is being installed before retainage is released.

Another important process is to photograph throughout all stages of construction. These should not be just snapshots of the home, but detailed documentation photos of construction. These photos can become very important references for future home additions, repairs, or structural issues that become a concern.

It is often worth the extra fees for an inspector to know that the work is quality and progressing as per specifications and contract agreements. An experienced inspector can pick up red flags or give alternative ideas that may not have been noticed during the original design process. However, be careful not to use this third party to constantly interfere with the other builders unless there are reasonable issues to address.

Resources

Blueprint Price Information

The plans in this book can be purchased from:

Beaver Creek Design Services

35 Territory Road
Oneida, NY 13421
www.beavercreekdesignservices.com
(315) 245-4112

Garage Plans:
5 Sets $325.00
8 Sets $375.00

Small Log Cabin Collection
(under 999 sq. ft.):
5 Sets $485.00
8 Sets $535.00

Log Home Storybook Collection
(1,000 to 1,999 sq. ft.):
5 Sets $745.00
8 Sets $796.00

Log Home Estate Collection
(2,000 to 2,999 sq. ft.):
5 Sets $845.00
8 Sets $895.00

*All prices are subject to change without notice.
All prices are subject to shipping and handling costs. Orders
should be made carefully. All plans are specifically printed
for each client with no refunds available.*

International Log Building Association

P.O. Box 775
Lumby, BC V0E 2G0
Canada
www.logassociation.org
(800) 532-2900
(250) 547-8776
(250) 547-8775 fax
*The Log Building Association website lists hundreds of tradi-
tional handcrafters from all over the world. Many listings are
not found in the standard log-building magazines.*

Log Home Guide

P.O. Box 671
1107 NW 4th Street
Grand Rapids, MN 55744-0671
www.loghomeguide.com
(888) 345-LOGS [5647]
*This special-issue magazine with a hand-selected list of the
top one hundred log and element builders in North America
has a valuable resource list of handcrafted log builders within
your region and around the world. This is not a list collected
by invitation only nor by paid advertisers.*

Crown Point Cabinetry

153 Charlestown Road
Claremont, NH 03743
(800) 999-4994
(800) 370-1218 fax
www.crown-point.com
Period-style cabinetry is handcrafted with the finest quality
finishes and within the tradition of master craftsmen and
artisans.

© 2003 Rob Melnychuk

Murray Arnott Design Ltd.
8 Saint Catharine Street
Guelph, ON N1H 4G3
www.designma.com
(519) 829-1758

Bead-and-Batten Doors
ATS Inc.
30 East Little Avenue
Driggs, ID 83422
(208) 456-2711
Traditional bead-and-batten and Z-back–style doors.

Bent-Wood of Chilson
225 Corduroy Road
Ticonderoga, NY 12883
(518) 597-3334

Carney Architects
P.O. Box 9218
Jackson, WY 83002
www.carneyarchitects.com
(307) 733-4000

Charles Cunniffe Architects
610 East Hyman Avenue
Aspen, CO 81611
www.cunniffe.com
(970) 925-5590

**Conklin's Authentic Antique Barnwood
and Hand-Hewn Beams**
RD #1, Box 70
Susquehanna, PA 18847
www.conklinsbarnwood.com
(570) 465-3832
Authentic antique barnwood and hand-hewn beams are
part of a new tradition of reclaiming and honoring the history
of wood.

Joslyn Fine Metalwork

1244 State Highway 80
Smyrna, NY 13464
www.usblacksmith.com
(607) 627-6580
(800) 985-9811
The art of metal craftsmanship is captured in every piece of metalwork, where detail and whimsy are incorporated into each unique sculpture.

Lake Placid Lodge

P.O. Box 550
Lake Placid, NY 12946
www.lakeplacidlodge.com
(518) 523-2700

Rita Dee

356 West Kerley Corners Road
Tivoli, NY 12583
(845) 757-5808
Artistic sculptures are created out of driftwood found on the shores of the Hudson River in New York.

Trout House Village Resort

9117 Lake Shore Drive
Hague, NY 12836
www.trouthouse.com
(800) 368-6088

HANDCRAFTED LOG BUILDERS THAT SPECIALIZE IN LOG-ELEMENT STRUCTURES

Ackerman Handcrafted Log Homes
P.O. Box 1318
Carbondale, CO 81623
www.ackermanloghomes.com
(970) 963-0119

Beaver Creek Log Homes
35 Territory Road
Oneida, NY 13421
www.beavercreekloghomes.com
(315) 245-4112

Custom Log Homes
P.O. Box 218, 3662 Hwy 93 North
Stevensville, MT 59870
www.customlog.com
(406) 777-5202

Frontier Builders Inc.
P.O. Box 389, 6373 Hwy 45 South
Land O'Lakes, WI 54540
www.fbiloghomes.com
(715) 547-6222

Hilgard Log Builders
P.O. Box 891
West Yellowstone, MT 59758
(406) 646-7234

John DeVries Log & Timber Homes
RR3
Tweed, Ontario KOK 3JO
www.johndevriesloghomes.com
(613) 478-6830

Maple Island Log Homes
5046 SW Bayshore Drive, Suite A
Suttons Bay, MI 49682
www.mapleisland.com
(800) 748-0137

Minde Log Construction, Inc.
2112 E. Pioneer Road
Duluth, MN 55806
www.mindelog.com
(218) 525-1070

Pedersen Logsmiths, Inc.
P.O. Box 788, Hwy 93 N
Challis, ID 83226
www.pedersenlogsmiths.com
(208) 879-4211

Sellman Log Structures, Inc.
24355 Esquire Boulevard
Forest Lake, MN 55025-5610
(651) 464-3843

The Wooden House Co.
3714 North Road
South Ryegate, VT 05069
(802) 429-2490

Timmerhus, Inc.
3000 N. 63rd Street
Boulder, CO 80301-2935
www.timmerhusinc.com
(303) 449-1336

Unique Timber Corp.
Box 730
Lumby, BC VOE 2G0
www.uniquetimber.com
(250) 547-2400